This Flag Never Goes Down!

40 Stories
of Confederate Battle Flags and
Color-Bearers at Gettysburg

by Michael Dreese

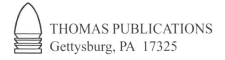

THOMAS PUBLICATIONS
Gettysburg, PA 17325

Printed and bound in the United States of America

Published by   THOMAS PUBLICATIONS
                P.O. Box 3031
                Gettysburg, Pa. 17325

ISBN-1-57747-102-4

Cover design by Ryan C. Stouch

Cover illustration, "The Boy Colonel." Painting by Don Troiani,
www.historicalartprints.com.

To the little "Rebels":
Brooke, Shane, Holly, Kristin, Brittany, Benjamin,
Karissa, and Lauren.

Preface

Being a native of Pennsylvania I have often displayed a predilection toward the North in my studies of the Civil War. Thus, when I struck upon the idea to compile a series of stories concerning the battle flags and color bearers at Gettysburg, it seemed natural to cover the Army of the Potomac first. Following the release of *Never Desert the Old Flag: 50 Stories of Union Battle Flags and Color-Bearers at Gettysburg* in the spring of 2002, I shifted gears and commenced my parallel study of the Army of Northern Virginia. A sense of freshness and wonderment immediately took hold—akin to walking down a familiar street in the opposite direction—the scenery remained the same, but the view changed dramatically.

At the same time, it became increasingly clear to me that the similarities between Union and Confederate soldiers far outweighed the differences. Both sides revered their flags and the principles and ideals that they embodied. In numerous cases men freely gave their lives to defend these banners from capture or dishonor. I was also fascinated by the unique sense of humor that pervaded the two armies under the most dire of circumstances.

From an economic standpoint it certainly behooves me to encourage readers to purchase both of my volumes on this subject. In addition to the very worthwhile result of adding to the coffers of my retirement fund, there is yet another compelling reason to do so—partisanship can severely limit one's understanding of virtually any historical topic.

Having made this statement, I should explain why I wrote ten fewer stories from the Confederate perspective. I can assure you that no slight was intended. First, primary and secondary sources on Southern regiments were not always readily available. In some cases, such as William Barksdale's Mississippi Brigade, they were virtually nonexistent. On the other hand, a wealth of information was available on George E. Pickett's Virginians. As a result, the coverage of Confederate units by brigades and divisions was less balanced than in my previous work.

A number of the stories that appear on these pages run a bit longer than those included in the Union edition. I also chose to present more introductory material in order to address some of the controversies surrounding the Confederate battle flag and to place them in the proper historical context. The reader will find a few extra flag vignettes in the chapter dealing with the campaign leading up to the battle and in the epilogue.

Because of my more limited exposure to the Confederate States of America, this volume was more research intensive than its Union counterpart. I count myself fortunate to live a little over an hour from the United States Military History Institute, Carlisle Barracks, Pennsylvania. I spent many hours there combing through the vast holdings of primary and secondary sources. The convenient unit bibliographies made my task much easier. Dr. Richard Sommers and the entire staff were very cordial and accommodating. I especially wish to thank JoAnna McDonald and Randy Hackenburg.

A large debt of gratitude is also due Ranger John Heiser for locating files and answering numerous questions during my visits to the Gettysburg National Military Park Library. I am fortunate to have him as a friend and value his knowledge of the battle.

My research was greatly enhanced by the previous work of fellow historians and authors. Of particular value were Kathy Georg Harrison's *Nothing But Glory: Pickett's Division at Gettysburg*, Richard Rollins' *"The Damned Red Flags of the Rebellion," The Confederate Battle Flag at Gettysburg*, Earl Hess' *Pickett's Charge — The Last Attack at Gettysburg*, and the definitive battle studies of Harry W. Pfanz.

William Mark Faucette, Carrollton, Georgia, provided detailed genealogical data on his ancestor, William F. Faucette. Wes Bradley kindly allowed me to include his photograph of Lieutenant Melvin Dwinnell.

I also wish to acknowledge the following individuals and organizations for providing copies of manuscripts or photographic images for this volume: Debbie Pendleton, Assistant Director for Public Services, Alabama Department of Archives and History, Montgomery, Alabama; Ian Lekus, Research Services, Rare Book, Manuscript, and Special Collections Library, Duke University, Durham, North Carolina; Steve Nielsen, Minnesota Historical Society, St. Paul, Minnesota; Jeffrey Rogers, Mississippi Department of Archives and History, Jackson, Mississippi; Michael Wright, Old Capitol Museum of Mississippi History, Jackson, Mississippi; Dr. Lenore Barbian, Assistant Curator of Anatomical Collections, Armed Forces Institute of Pathology, National Museum of Health and Medicine, Washington, D. C.; Steve Massengill, North Carolina Department of Cultural Resources, Raleigh, North Carolina; Lisa Kobrin, Reference Librarian, Central North Carolina Regional Library, Burlington, North Carolina; Susan Gordon, Archivist, Tennessee State Library and Archives, Nashville, Tennessee; Stephen D. Cox, Photographic Archives Manager, Tennessee State Museum, Nashville, Tennessee.

This volume would have been incomplete without the cooperation of the following staff members of the Museum of the Confederacy, Richmond, Virginia: Rebecca A. Rose, Curator of the Flag Collection; Cara Griggs, Research Assistant; and Heather Milne, Manager of Photographic Collections. Numbering over 500, the Museum houses the largest single collection of Confederate national, state, presentation, company, and regimental flags. The institution's Flag Conservation Program deserves the support of all interested individuals and organizations. With its comprehensive collection of artifacts and exhibits, a visit to this museum is a required pilgrimage for all aficionados of the Confederacy.

As with my past projects I thank my friends Pete Wilson, Williamsport, Pa., Tim Smith, Gettysburg, Pa., and Garry Adelman, Germantown, Md., for reading over my manuscript and making valuable corrections and insights.

Kudos to the entire team at Thomas Publications for their support and encouragement, including Dean Thomas, Jim Thomas, Sally Thomas, Truman Eyler, Kay Eyler, and Andy DeCusati.

Finally, no writer can succeed without the understanding of his or her family. My love goes out to my wife, Heather, and my children, Brooke and Shane. Thanks for tolerating the incurable obsessions of a history fanatic.

Furl that Banner, softly, slowly;
Treat it gently — it is holy,
For it droops above the dead;
Touch it not — unfold it never;
Let it droop there, furled forever,
For its peoples' hopes are fled.

—Abram Joseph Ryan

Introduction

Perhaps no symbol in American history has generated as much passionate debate as the Confederate battle flag. Indeed, the familiar, star-studded, blue St. Andrew's cross on a red field divides Americans almost as much today as it did 140 years ago. Actually, the flag itself is not the root cause of this dissension, but rather the perception of what it represents. Blacks, as well as many whites, view the banner as a reminder of slavery and racial oppression. This image has been proliferated by white supremacist groups such as the Ku Klux Klan, the Aryan Nation, and anti-government militia groups, who have adopted the symbol to advance their movements.

But to many white Southerners, the flag symbolizes the valor of those who fought to secure their freedom from a tyrannical Federal government that was out of touch with their distinctive way of life. According to Shelby Foote, the popular Southern historian and novelist, the critics who believe the flag represents slavery are grossly oversimplifying the matter. "It stood for law, honor, love of country," he maintained.[1] Foote is angry that hate groups have distorted the true meaning of the flag, but he is also sympathetic toward their victims. "I really do understand the pain that an intelligent black feels when he sees the Confederate flag, because...back in the '60s and '70s, [it] was carried by yahoos who represented everything that had held them down and abused them."[2]

These latent issues bubbled to the surface during the recent flag controversies in South Carolina, Georgia, and Mississippi. In what was dubbed, "the last battle of the Civil War," the two camps fought over the Confederate flag that had flown over the dome of the State House in Columbia, South Carolina, since 1962 in defiance of forced desegregation. Civil rights groups, led by the NAACP, argued that the flag served as a constant reminder that the hatred and divisiveness that marked this tumultuous period still exist. They launched an economic boycott and organized marches and demonstrations to force the removal of the offensive banner. On January 17, 2000, nearly 50,000 people attended a rally in Columbia on Martin Luther King, Jr. Day to protest the flying of the flag.

Southern heritage groups such as the Sons of Confederate Veterans and the League of the South countered with their own demonstrations and a vigorous publicity campaign. They argued that slavery thrived under the United States flag from 1776-1865, but only four years under the Confederacy. It was also pointed out that both banners originated during a violent struggle for independence and self-rule. The debate leapt upon the national stage during the 2000 presidential campaign. Vice-president Al Gore called for the removal of the flag while Pat Buchanan of the Reform Party defended its presence. The Republican candidates, George W. Bush, John McCain, and Steve Forbes, initially ducked the controversial issue by declaring that it was up to the voters of the state to decide.

Finally, after months of impassioned debate, the South Carolina Legislature voted to remove the flag from the capitol dome. Its lowering on July 1, 2000, marked the end of an era. As a concession to heritage organizations, the politicians permitted the flag to be displayed near a Confederate memorial on the grounds of the state house. This solution did not appease members of the NAACP who continue to demand that the banner be removed from the property completely.

Then, in February 2001, Florida Governor Jeb Bush ordered the removal of the "Stainless Banner," the second national flag of the Confederacy, from the capitol's west entrance in Tallahassee. At the same time, the emblems commemorating the French, Spanish, and British governments that once ruled the state were also retired. Bush spokesperson Katie Baur defended the action by pointing out that, "Regardless of our views about the symbolism of the...flags...the governor believes...that the symbols of Florida's past should not be displayed in a manner that may divide Floridians today."[3] Although the removal of the flags did not spark widespread protest, some critics perceived it as a knee-jerk reaction to political correctness.

At present four Southern states, Alabama, Arkansas, Georgia, and Mississippi, still incorporate elements of the Confederate battle flag into the design of their state flags. The Peach State legislators added the icon in 1956, two years after the U. S. Supreme Court ruled against segregation in public schools. In January 2001, after months of rancorous debate, Georgia lawmakers agreed to shrink the emblem but not remove it from the flag as part of a new design.

Three months later, Mississippi voters decided to retain the Confederate symbol on their flag by a margin of 65-35 percent, rejecting the pleas of prominent political and business leaders that a less controversial design would encourage investment and bolster the state's lagging economy. In January 2002, Kenneth Stokes, a city councilman in Jackson, staged a protest outside the capitol building to encourage the state legislature to override the vote. As the celebrated writer William Faulkner once wrote of his native Mississippi, "The past is never dead."[4]

During these disputes, editorial cartoonists enjoyed limitless fodder for their creations. One caricature featured a confrontation between a white man and a black man. Pointing to his Rebel flag T-shirt, the pot-bellied good old boy exclaims, "My people died because of this flag." His adversary coolly responds, "So did mine." Another cartoon replaces the thirteen stars on the Confederate flag with miniature hooded clansmen. But perhaps the most striking depiction is that of a white, middle-aged businessman being crucified upon the St. Andrew's cross. Across his dress shirt is printed, "South Carolina's future."[5]

Efforts to eradicate the Confederate battle flag have percolated down to all aspects of American life. School districts across the country have prohibited its display on apparel and on student vehicles, prompting debate on freedom of expression rights. The "Rebels" of one Southern high school now wave a "spirit" flag at sporting events in lieu of the tarnished battle flag. The Sons of Confederate Veterans have brought legal suits in several states over the right to display the emblem on specialty license plates. The group has emerged victorious in several states, including Maryland, Virginia, and North Carolina.[6]

But despite all of the bad press, or perhaps as a result of it, the de facto symbol of the defunct Confederacy continues to flourish. Hundreds of web sites and numerous books and articles are devoted to the interpretation of its meaning and significance, both pro and con. Once reserved for memorial rituals and monument dedications, the flag has been transformed into a part of American popular culture. One Internet merchandiser offers a wide variety of items featuring the logo — T-shirts, Afghans, ball caps, beach towels, and even bikinis! Tattoos are the ultimate choice for those who wish to permanently display their devotion.

Why the popularity? The purchasers of such items certainly risk being labeled as racists, or at the least rednecks. However, it appears that many of them view the icon as a symbol of rugged American individualism, resistance to authority, or as an expression of their adventuresome personality. It is doubtful that more than a handful of these devotees have any grasp of the origin and history of the flag they so proudly display. Even those who possess such knowledge, however, usually adopt a narrow stance and are rarely sympathetic to the views of the other side. But then the Confederate battle flag is rarely viewed in shades of gray. (Excuse the pun).

If a Confederate veteran could be resurrected long enough to witness a modern debate on the flag, he might inquire as to what all the fuss was about. In fact, if he was among the nearly 400 Southern-ers killed in action at the Battle of Bull Run on July 21, 1861, the war's first major encounter, he would not even recognize what we refer to today as the Confederate battle flag!

Following the inauguration of Jefferson Davis as president of the newly formed Confederate States of America in February 1861, hun-dreds of designs were submitted for a flag to represent the new gov-ernment. Because the citizens of the South shared a common heritage as well as many of the same values as their northern neighbors, it is not surprising that the first national flag of the Confederacy closely resembled the Stars and Stripes. The Stars and Bars featured three horizontal stripes of equal width in alternating bands of red, white, and red. One star representing each state formed a circle on a blue field in the canton. The number of stars varied depending upon the period of manufacture.

C.S.A. Flag, First National Pattern, commonly know as the "Stars and Bars."
The flag pictured here was taken from a home in north Alabama by a Federal
soldier.   Courtesy of Alabama Department of Archives and History

The similarity with the United States flag caused a great deal of confusion for both sides during the opening clash at Bull Run. Thus, Confederate generals P. G. T. Beauregard and Joseph E. Johnston decided that a distinct battle flag was needed to avoid misidentification in future battles. Beauregard consulted Congressman William Porcher Mills, the chairman of the Committee on Flag and Seal. Mills suggested a design he had submitted earlier for consideration as the national flag—a rectangular blue St. Andrew's cross or saltier, upon which a five-pointed star was affixed for each state, on a red field. Both commanders approved though Johnston insisted that the pattern be altered into a square shape of about four feet.

With minor variations this banner remained the standard issue for what would become known as the Army of Northern Virginia throughout the remainder of the war. The first flags of the new design were made of silk. When this material became scarce it was replaced by wool bunting, much of it imported from England. Depending on the time of issue, the border could be yellow, orange, or white and the number of stars could be either twelve or thirteen.[7]

Although the creation of the new battle flag was an important measure in creating a degree of uniformity within the South's premiere fighting force in the Eastern Theater, the Confederate government never authorized this flag as the official battle standard for all of its various field armies. As a result, efforts at standardization met with only limited success in other Eastern armies, and the flags carried by Western commands were even more eclectic. For example, no fewer than eight different designs could be observed within the Army of Tennessee in 1863.[8]

Not even all of the units within the Army of Northern Virginia strictly adhered to the new mandate. A few regiments continued to carry the Stars and Bars while others used banners designed to replicate state or local patterns. Both Virginia and North Carolina issued their own distinctive battle flags, but these standards were usually reserved for special occasions and were not typically carried into combat.

The Southern Cross was also incorporated into the design of the Second National flag. Adopted in May 1863, the "Stainless Banner" consisted of a white field with the new battle flag in the canton. Near the end of the war, a red vertical band was attached to the fly end to avoid confusion with a flag of surrender.

C.S.A. Flag, Third National Pattern. *The Second National Pattern or "Stainless Banner" was similar in appearance except for the red bar at the fly end.* Courtesy of Alabama Department of Archives and History

Although never officially sanctioned by the Confederate government, the Bonnie Blue Flag was perhaps the most beloved of all Southern flags. The simple design of a single white star on a blue field first appeared in 1810 as the emblem of the short-lived Republic of West Florida. It resurfaced in the late 1830s as the official flag of the Republic of Texas, and for several weeks in 1861, it flew over the Republic of Mississippi. In one form or another, the lone star was adopted into the designs of five state flags in 1861.[9]

That same year Arkansas comedian Henry McCarthy composed his famous ballad, "The Bonnie Blue Flag," a song surpassed only by "Dixie" in the hearts of the Southern people. The last stanza typified the sacrifice of Southern soldiers throughout the war: "Then here's to our Confederacy, strong we are and brave, Like patriots of old, we'll fight our heritage to save; And rather than submit to shame, to die we would prefer, So cheer for the Bonnie Blue Flag that bears a Single Star."[10]

In camp, on the march, and most importantly, in combat, battle flags served as a constant reminder of this pledge. The deep sentiments evoked by these icons are well illustrated in a flag presentation ceremony that took place in New Orleans in 1861. As she presented the new colors to the assembled troops, the head seamstress implored the men that "when this bright flag shall float before you on the battlefield, let it not only inspire you with the brave and patriotic ambition of a soldier aspiring to his own and the country's honor and glory, but also may it be a sign that cherished ones appeal to you to save them from a fanatical and heartless foe."

Upon receiving the flag, the color sergeant vowed "that no stain shall ever be found upon thy sacred folds, save the blood of those who attack thee or those who fall in thy defense." He then addressed his comrades, "In the smoke, glare, and din of battle, amidst carnage and death, there let its bright folds inspire you with new strength, nerve your arms and steel your hearts to deeds of strength and valor."[11]

Four years of unprecedented death and suffering could not extinguish this devotion. Union General Joshua Chamberlain recalled the somber surrender ceremony at Appomattox in April 1865 where each Confederate regiment stacked arms and "reluctantly, with agony of expression, they tenderly folded their flags, battle-worn and torn, bloodstained, heart-holding colors, and laid them down."[12]

What factors influenced this undying bond? The answer is complex and multilayered. For both Northern and Southern soldiers, the flags carried onto the field of battle represented the ideals and values they strove to uphold. It cannot be denied that some of the men who wore gray fought to preserve the institution of slavery. One officer from Mississippi told his wife in 1863 that "this country without slave labor would be completely worthless.... If the negroes are freed the country...is not worth fighting for.... We can only live and exist by that species of labor: and hence I am willing to continue to fight to the last."[13] However, only about twenty percent of white families owned slaves in 1860.

Indeed, the vast majority of Southern volunteers believed they were fighting to secure *their liberty* from an oppressive central government that was bent on imposing its will and values upon them. Inspired by their Revolutionary forefathers, they argued that the Constitution guaranteed them the right to secede from the Union if they so chose. States' rights and individual self-reliance formed the core of Southern society.

Unlike modern military units, Civil War companies were recruited and organized at the local level. Thus, the new recruit marched off to war with people he knew — friends, neighbors, and often relatives. When these scattered companies were joined together to form a regiment, their battle flag fused them together. The banners became a great source of pride to these large extended families and represented everything they had shared — victories, lost comrades, toilsome marches, and privations — experiences that were universal, but also singular to each unit. The regiment was the basic Civil war fighting unit. Originally composed of about 1,000 men, casualties and attrition often reduced the strength of veteran units to several hundred members.[14]

In addition to its state and numerical designation each regiment painted its accumulated battle honors upon their standard. These markings accented with bullet holes and bloodstains told the story of a unit's history more forcefully than words could ever do.

There were additional meanings more individualistic in nature. The flag represented a soldier's family, his community, and his religious beliefs. Fighting under its folds, he also believed that his personal honor, courage, and sense of duty were being tested. All of these influences combined to transform a swath of fabric into a powerful motivational tool.[15]

In addition to their symbolic importance, battle flags served a number of utilitarian functions. Because of their large size, rear echelon commanders could monitor the movement of troops from a safe distance. This quality became increasingly important following the opening stages of an engagement. After a few volleys were exchanged, the battlefield was often shrouded in a low-lying cloud of acrid smoke produced by the discharge of hundreds of muzzleloading rifles. Hoisted on wooden staffs at least eight feet in length, the brightly colored banners were often the only visible elements of the contending forces.

The flags were even more vital to front line officers and to the men in the ranks. Nineteenth century combat was characterized by mass movements of troops in compact formations, the primary objective being the concentration of a heavy volume of fire against the weakest portion of the enemy line.

As a regiment advanced in line of battle, its color bearer, positioned near the center of the formation, stepped off several paces ahead of the other troops. Since everyone guided upon him, it was essential that the color sergeant preserve the proper length and cadence of the march while orienting the line in the proper direction.[16] In the deadly close-quarters combat that ensued, the sight of the flag floating above the chaos steeled the resolve of the infantrymen. If the line gave way or if a retreat was ordered, the men halted upon the command to "rally around the colors." Physical stamina, unflinching courage, and leadership skill were requisite qualities of a good color bearer.

Naturally, the visibility of battle flags also made them a convenient reference point for enemy riflemen. Just before being severely wounded at Gettysburg, one Union soldier recalled, "The last thing I remember seeing was the rebel flag and I was shot just as I was leveling my gun to fire at the enemy."[17] Remarkably, the color bearer did not carry a weapon. The protection of the flag was the sole responsibility of the two to nine man color guard, who like the bearer were chosen for their bravery and steadiness.[18]

If the color sergeant was shot down a member of his escort immediately picked up the flag. Soldiers often vied for this post of honor despite the inherent risk. Because flags were the focal point of Civil War combat, the casualty rates of the color party and of the companies clustered nearby were usually significantly higher than those incurred by units positioned farther from the colors.

Because of their emotional appeal and vital function, losing a stand of colors was considered a terrible disgrace. Indeed, it was almost considered sacrilegious to allow the flag to touch the ground. On the other hand, a captured enemy flag was a highly prized trophy. The loss or capture of a standard almost always received attention in the official reports filed by commanders. Civil War color-bearers often resorted to drastic measures to save their flags from capture. Many choose to tear the fabric into small pieces or even to lay down their lives rather than surrender the pride of the regiment to the opposition.[19]

Pride and reverence for the battle flag swelled to new heights within the Army of Northern Virginia during the late spring of 1863. Under its beloved leader, General Robert E. Lee, the army had chalked up an impressive string of victories against its chief nemesis, the numerically superior and better equipped Army of the Potomac. High morale and confidence abounded. One officer wrote of Lee, "We looked forward to victory under him as confidently as to successive sunrises."[20] Another boasted, "I have little doubt that we had now the finest army ever marshaled on this side of the Atlantic, and one scarcely inferior to any Europe has known."[21]

Not only did the Battle of Gettysburg shatter these claims of invincibility, it also represented the zenith of Southern hopes for an independent nation. Although Lee's men would fight tenaciously for nearly two more years, their fortunes would never burn as brightly after those fateful three days in July 1863.

The landmark battle also represented the genesis of a new era in warfare. Upon the gently rolling hills and fields of southern Pennsylvania, the respective commanders received another painful reminder that technological advances in weaponry and projectiles called for new tactics. Thus, the grand pageantry of Pickett's Charge gradually gave way to the grinding monotony of trench warfare at Petersburg, which was in turn a precursor of the Western Front in World War I. More modern modes of warfare eventually spelled the end for the chivalrous color bearer, the very embodiment of the Victorian concepts of duty, honor, and courage.

In the following pages the reader will step back in time and view the Confederate battle flag from the perspective of the men who fought under it in one of the most pivotal battles of the American Civil War. Hopefully, he or she will be enthralled by these stories of sacrifice and devotion while gaining a new appreciation and an increased tolerance for a symbol that has been both misused and unfairly maligned by modern America.

But as John Coski, historian at the Museum of the Confederacy in Richmond, Virginia, pointed out, "The Confederate battle flag will continue to be what it has been for almost half a century: a contentious symbol that reflects accurately America's divided mind over the origins, life, and legacies of the Confederacy."[22]

The Campaign

By the spring of 1863 military funerals had become commonplace in the Confederate capital of Richmond, Virginia. The ceremony that took place in the city on May 12, 1863, was a remarkable exception. As the sharp crack of a signal gun echoed through the still morning air near the equestrian statue of George Washington, a hearse drawn by a quartet of white horses slowly pulled away from the Governor's Mansion. By order of President Jefferson Davis the metallic coffin it bore was draped with the very first issue of the new national flag approved just ten days earlier by the Congress of the Confederate States of America. The snow-white field of the "Stainless Banner" was nearly covered with flowers deposited by the grief-stricken daughters of the South. General George E. Pickett and staff preceded the hearse with a contingent of infantry, cavalry, and artillery. Directly behind it a servant led the decorated war-horse of the fallen warrior. Now the saddle contained only the boots last worn by the rider. Behind the steed marched the staff of the former officer with a group of convalescent soldiers that he had once commanded in the heat of battle. Next in line were a vast array of dignitaries: President Davis, members of his Cabinet, leading army and naval officers, city officials, and finally, the heart-broken family members and relatives of the deceased.

The solemn mile-long procession crept south along Governor Street, veered to the right at the junction with Main Street, then after marching ten blocks, returned to Capitol Square via Second Street and Grace Street. All business had been suspended and the entire route was lined with weeping admirers. An even denser throng of onlookers awaited the pageant near the western entrance of the square. As a band played a mournful dirge the hearse passed underneath a canopy of stately trees and through a carpet of vivid green lawns before halting at the steps of the capitol. At this point the pallbearers, who included Generals James Longstreet, Richard Ewell, George Pickett, Richard Garnett, and James Kemper, carried the coffin into the Hall of the House of Representatives. It was placed upon a catafalque covered with white linen, and draped with bows of crepe, in front of the Speaker's chair.[1]

It was an unseasonably warm spring day, but over twenty thousand people waited patiently in the sweltering heat to file into the chambers for a final glimpse of the hero idol of the South. Richmond resident Sallie Putnam expressed the opinion that the predominately white flag characterized the stainless reputation of the man who lay underneath its folds — "a fit emblem of his own pure spirit and the sublime courage with which he bore his Master's cross."[2]

After midnight when the great crowds had finally dissipated, Henry Kyd Douglas, a youthful member of the slain officer's staff walked alone to the Capitol. After being admitted by the sentinels, he viewed his old chief by the faint light of flickering candles. He noted the cold white face that appeared as firm as marble accented by the sharp, chiseled nose, the high forehead, and the tightly closed lips. "There was no voice to respond to a good-bye," lamented Henry, "I picked up a few flowers and took my last leave of Stonewall Jackson." In his memoirs Douglas summarized the death of Lieutenant General Thomas J. "Stonewall" Jackson as "the heart-break of the Southern Confederacy."[3]

Perhaps no one felt the loss as deeply as did the commander of the Army of Northern Virginia. But General Robert E. Lee had precious little time to mourn the loss of his dear friend and chief lieutenant. On the day prior to the funeral Lee could not leave his Fredericksburg headquarters long enough to ride to the train depot as Jackson's remains were being placed upon the cars. There was simply too much work to be done.

Lee had just achieved the most brilliant success of his illustrious career. In the tangled woodlands surrounding the tiny crossroads of Chancellorsville, he had boldly intercepted a well-conceived offensive by Union General Joseph Hooker. Dividing his army in the face of a superior foe, Lee unleashed Jackson on a devastating flank attack. But at the height of his success, Stonewall was cut down by friendly fire at dusk on May 2, 1863. Eight days later, he succumbed to pneumonia. The defeated Army of the Potomac retreated to the opposite side of the Rappahannock and returned to its old camps near Falmouth.

The triumph was a hollow one from the Southern viewpoint. Besides Jackson, Lee's army had suffered a proportionately higher number of casualties than its opponent, including a staggering number of officers. And the strategic situation had not changed. A powerful

Federal army lay poised on the opposite side of the river as it had for nearly six months. Hooker could resume the offensive at any time. In light of this fact, Lee believed that the time was ripe for his long-anticipated invasion of the North. The country around the Rappahannock had been greatly depleted of food and forage during the long occupation by the two armies. Thus, Lee had cast a covetous eye toward the rich farmlands of the Cumberland Valley in southern Pennsylvania. Also, by seizing the initiative he could thwart Hooker's plans for a summer campaign and hopefully relieve some of the pressure from Vicksburg, Mississippi, which lay under siege by Union forces under Ulysses S. Grant.

Lee also had some larger goals in mind. After capturing the state capital of Harrisburg, a major rail center, he planned to advance upon a large seaboard city such as Philadelphia or Baltimore. By occupying Northern territory he hoped to agitate the growing anti-war movement there and also gain official recognition from England and France. Perhaps then he could secure a negotiated peace favorable to the Confederacy.[4]

Before Lee launched his invasion, he made some overdue changes. The most important of these reforms involved reorganizing his two unwieldy infantry corps into three smaller ones. Lieutenant General James Longstreet retained command of the veteran First Corps. A. P. Hill, one of the army's most aggressive division commanders, received the reins of the newly created Third Corps. For Jackson's old Second Corps, Lee tapped 46-year-old Richard S. Ewell, who had performed brilliantly under Stonewall's watchful eye during the legendary Valley Campaign of 1862.

Within a month of Chancellorsville Lee had attended to the myriad preparations required for his invasion. By June 4, two-thirds of his army had slipped away from their old lines. General Hill's Third Corps remained behind to hold the Federal troops in place for as long as possible.[5]

Lee's troops marched west, then swung north down the Shenandoah Valley behind the shielding heights of the Blue Ridge Mountains. Because of his familiarity with the region, Ewell was selected to lead the advance. His first mission was to clear out a Union garrison at Winchester commanded by General Robert H. Milroy. This outpost was situated at the northern terminus of the Valley and lay directly in the path of the invasion.

Courtesy of Pete Wilson

Lt. General Richard S. Ewell

Ewell confused his opponent with diversions and then launched a surprise attack on June 14. The unsuspecting defenders were pushed back into their inner defenses. During the early morning hours of the next day, Milroy attempted to extricate his forces from the encircling snare. At dawn the Confederates ambushed the fleeing Union troops at Stephenson's Depot. As Milroy tried to cut his way out, Ewell's men scooped up a large number of prisoners. The Union commander and the remnants of his shattered force retreated to the security of Harpers Ferry.

As the fighting roared north of town, a Confederate brigade led by Brigadier General John B. Gordon seized the main Federal fort without firing a shot. Elated, the general hauled down the Stars and Stripes from the flagpole, then attached it to his saddle with the rope section and dashed off in triumph. Afterward, a makeshift Confederate flag fashioned by the ladies of Winchester from captured U. S. flags was hoisted up the pole. After a symbolic salute of thirteen guns, the large earthen structure formerly known as the Flag Fort or Main Fort was christened "Fort Jackson" by Ewell in honor of his fallen mentor.[6]

Having suffered under the oppressive reign of the brutish Milroy for six months, the occupants of the town had been eagerly anticipating this day. The admiring ladies called on Ewell to make a speech. The modest commander demurred. Pulling rank, he brought forward Major General Jubal Early, his senior division commander, citing his subordinate's speaking experience as a prewar lawyer. Thinking quickly, the bachelor Early devised a clever and charming escape clause. "Ladies," he announced, "I never could find courage to address one of you — of course I can't speak to a hundred."[7]

Ewell was not content to rest on his laurels. By the evening of June 15, his lead division under Major General Robert Rodes crossed the Potomac River near Williamsport, Maryland. Only raw militia stood in the path of Lee's vanguard and panic spread throughout southern Pennsylvania.

Lee now had assurance that his new Second Corps commander would prove to be a worthy replacement for Jackson. With the Valley cleared of Federal resistance, the army chief ordered General A. P. Hill to abandon his old position and follow in the wake of Ewell and Longstreet.

As regiment after regiment of Hill's rag-tag veterans filed into line, one unit stood out from the rest. With about 850 men, the 26th North Carolina was the largest regiment in the Army of Northern Virginia at the time, outnumbering some brigades. It might also have been the most martial. One of its members recalled: "What a fine appearance the regiment made as it marched out from its bivouac near Fredericksburg that beautiful June morning. The men beaming in their splendid uniforms; the colors flying, and the drums beating; everything seemed propitious of success."[8]

Perhaps no one viewed the scene with as much optimism as the 26th's youthful colonel, 21-year-old Henry King Burgwyn, Jr. As he watched Sergeant Jefferson B. Mansfield hoist the regiment's newly issued Army of Northern Virginia battle flag, Burgwyn could envision the glory he and his men would win under its folds in the coming campaign. Although the 26th had experienced combat during the early part of its service, the regiment had been relegated to guard duty in the Petersburg, Virginia, area as Lee's army won successive victories at Second Manassas, Fredericksburg, and Chancellorsville. The ambitious Burgwyn chafed under the inactivity. By the time he took over the reins of the 26th in August of

1862, he was already the youngest colonel in the army, but the "Boy Colonel" had his sights set on a general's star. The son of a wealthy North Carolina planter, Henry received an excellent education. After failing in several attempts to gain admittance to West Point, he enrolled at the University of North Carolina in 1857. Two years later, after earning his Bachelor of Science degree, the 17-year-old scholar was accepted at the prestigious Virginia Military Institute in Lexington with advanced standing. In letters to the superintendent of the institution, Henry King Burgwyn, Sr. expressed concern over his son's reticent nature and his frail physical condition. He need not have worried. Through hard work and diligence, Burgwyn ranked second in a class of seventeen by the start of his senior year in 1861.

The VMI class of 1861 received their diplomas early; the graduates rushed to Richmond in late April as war fever erupted throughout the country. Accompanying Cadet Burgwyn was a personal note of endorsement addressed to the secretary of war from one Thomas J. Jackson, the professor of natural philosophy, who observed great potential in his former pupil.[9]

The soldiers of the 26th North Carolina also learned to look past their new leader's aristocratic airs and his strict attention to discipline. One member described him as "a youth of authority, beautiful and handsome; the flash of his eye and the quickness of his movements betokened his bravery. At first sight I both feared and admired him."[10] Another soldier recalled years later, "He was always cool under fire and knew exactly what to do, and his men were devoted to him."[11]

As Lee's army swung north, Henry penned a letter to his mother that brimmed with confidence. He closed, however, with a cautionary note: "What will be the result of the movements now on foot God alone can tell. I hope to be able to do my duty to the best of my ability & leave the result to His infinite wisdom & justice. Whatever may be my own fate I...feel & believe that all will turn out for the best."[12]

Although these words could be viewed as a premonition, Burgwyn was already looking ahead to peacetime. He planned to wed his sweetheart Anne Devereux, a 19-year-old Raleigh beauty and settle down into a planter's life. In anticipation of Southern Independence, Harry urged his father to put every spare cent he had toward purchasing slaves, particularly young females. He speculated that each would be worth from $2,000 to $3,000 six months after the war.[13] But before any dreams could be fulfilled, a difficult trial lay ahead in Pennsylvania.

Through a combination of wise planning and good fortune, Lee's army gained a head start of several days on the 90,000-man Army of the Potomac. In order to keep between the Confederates and Washington, D. C., General Hooker pushed his troops relentlessly northward on a parallel course. By the middle of the month the exhausted Union foot soldiers had reached the Centreville area about twenty miles west of the capital. As his infantrymen rested, Hooker directed his cavalry chief to push his troopers toward the Blue Ridge Mountains to gain information on the location of the enemy.[14]

For five days the sound of thundering hooves, the sharp crack of pistols and carbines, and the metallic clanging of sabers shattered the bucolic landscape of the Loudoun Valley as the Union cavalry clashed with their Southern counterparts led by the dashing cavalier, Major General James Ewell Brown "Jeb" Stuart. Although the Yankee horsemen pushed their adversaries back to the foot of the Blue Ridge, they failed to penetrate Stuart's protective screen.

Near the hamlet of Upperville on June 21, the 9th Virginia Cavalry was nearly surrounded by blue troopers during a rear guard action. As the Virginians cut through the trap, they engaged in a swirling hand-to-hand melee.[15]

The ladies of Lancaster County had presented Company D with a blue, gold-fringed silk flag, emblazoned with the Virginia state seal and motto. The inscriptions, "Our Troop" and "God and Your Native Land," were stitched on the one side. While carrying these colors, Bugler William Chichester Tapscott received a mortal wound. His brother, Lieutenant Aulbin Tapscott, allowed himself to be captured so that he could be with his dying sibling. William passed away that evening in a nearby home. After attending to his brother's burial, Aulbin took the flag out of William's knapsack, where it had been concealed, and wrapped it around his body underneath his uniform to prevent its capture.[16]

Within a week of the cavalry clash at Upperville, Hill's and Longstreet's Corps splashed across the Potomac River to the accompaniment of "Maryland! My Maryland" and "The Bonnie Blue Flag." After crossing the Mason Dixon Line, Lee established army headquarters at Chambersburg, Pennsylvania. As the bulk of the army concentrated in this area, Richard Ewell continued to carry out his

Obverse view of the battle flag carried by Company D
9th Virginia Cavalry, the "Lancaster Cavalry."
Courtesy of the Museum of the Confederacy, Richmond, Va. Photo by Katherine Wetzel

independent mission. His new orders were to advance into the heart of Pennsylvania to collect food and supplies.

General Early's Division marched eastward across South Mountain, brushed aside a raw militia regiment near Gettysburg on June 26, and then captured the city of York two days later. Meanwhile, Ewell continued northeast up the Cumberland Valley with the remaining two divisions. As his main body of troops camped around Carlisle on June 27, the corps commander sent a detachment of cavalry to scout the approaches to Harrisburg, which lay less than thirty miles to the northeast. Rodes' Division camped on the grounds of the U. S. Army Barracks, where Ewell himself had been stationed for a period prior to the war. Ewell and Rodes set up headquarters in one of the officer's residences.[17]

Sunday, June 28, was a day of rest and celebration for Ewell's jubilant men. Discovering a number of U. S. garrison flags at the barracks, Major Campbell Brown and some other staff officers decided "to raise a Confederate flag for the benefit of the ignorant citizens." By request, several local tailors created a Second National Flag by utilizing the battle flag of the 32nd North Carolina as the canton and attaching the white stripes from the confiscated flags. The homemade banner was hoisted up the post flagstaff and unfurled to the breeze.[18]

One Tarheel proudly proclaimed that "it was the flag of one of their regiments that waved defiantly on the enemy's soil at a point farther north than any other Confederate flag during the whole war."[19] He and his comrades were treated to a delightful afternoon of speech-making and enthusiastic rejoicing.

Suffering from a severe headache, Ewell said a few words to the assembled troops, then retired to his quarters. But unlike the ceremony held two weeks earlier at Winchester, plenty of willing orators appeared. By this time a number of officers were feeling "quite jolly" from the effects of a keg of lager beer that had been discovered on the premises. The potency of the brew was enhanced by the addition of some local whiskey.[20]

General Rodes delivered "a short, neat speech" from a nearby balcony and was followed by Brigadier General Junius Daniel. Afterwards, Major General Isaac Trimble, who was serving as a volunteer aide to Ewell, took center stage and "made a few remarks not so very neat." Major Brown noted that all three men were suffering from various states of intoxication. When the men shouted for another speech, Benjamin Green, the corps inspector, stepped forward. Green was so incoherent that he had to be pulled away twice and eventually put to bed.[21] One soldier later reflected that these light-hearted scenes stood in sharp contrast to the unspeakable horrors they would witness at Gettysburg just three days later.[22]

Major General Isaac Trimble
Courtesy of the Library of Congress

As the celebration was winding down in Carlisle, General Lee received a disturbing piece of intelligence from a spy who found his way to army headquarters near Chambersburg — the Army of the Potomac was concentrating at Frederick, Maryland, less than forty miles to the south. The general had been under the impression that the Yankee army had not yet crossed the Potomac.

Alarmed by the proximity of the enemy, Lee immediately issued a set of orders that would reunite his scattered 75,000 troops. He ordered a concentration near Cashtown, a large pass in South Mountain located eight miles west of Gettysburg. On this same day George Gordon Meade replaced Hooker as commander of the Army of the Potomac.

The news that Ewell received from army headquarters the following day did nothing to relieve his headache. The general dutifully abandoned his advance on Harrisburg and turned southward. He also ordered Early back from York. Meanwhile, the rest of Lee's army led by A. P. Hill's Corps marched east along the Chambersburg Pike toward the assembly point.

From his advanced position near the mountain pass, Hill sent out a reconnaissance toward Gettysburg on June 30. For this assignment he chose Brigadier General James J. Pettigrew's Brigade of North Carolina troops. As Pettigrew approached the western edge of the town during mid-morning, he learned that a body of Union cavalry was approaching Gettysburg from the south. Under strict orders not to bring on an engagement, Pettigrew instead ordered an immediate countermarch. When he returned from his mission neither his division commander, Major General Henry Heth, nor Hill could be convinced that any portion of the Army of the Potomac had reached Gettysburg. They insisted that the approaching force must have been home guard cavalry or militia troops instead. Near the end of the meeting, Heth turned to Hill and asked if he had any objection to marching his division into Gettysburg the next day. "None in the world," Hill replied.[23]

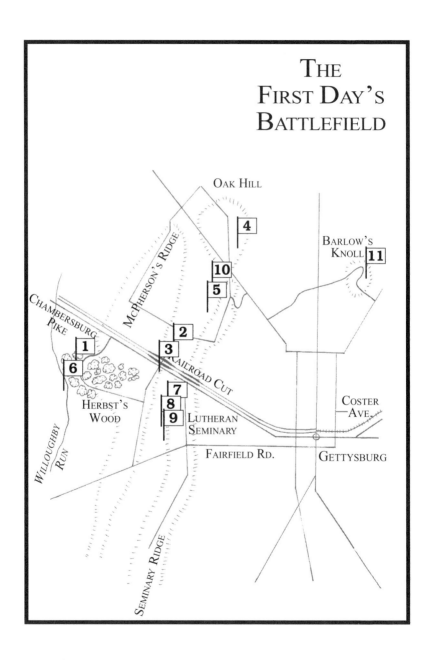

THE
FIRST DAY'S
BATTLEFIELD

OAK HILL

BARLOW'S
KNOLL

CHAMBERSBURG PIKE

McPHERSON'S RIDGE

RAILROAD CUT

HERBST'S
WOOD

WILLOUGHBY RUN

LUTHERAN
SEMINARY

COSTER
AVE.

FAIRFIELD RD.

GETTYSBURG

SEMINARY RIDGE

July 1, 1863

General Henry Heth had his division on the road by 5 a.m. on July 1. The brigades of Generals James Archer and Joseph Davis led the way, followed by Pettigrew's North Carolinians, with Colonel John Brockenbrough's Virginians bringing up the rear. Major General William Dorsey Pender's hard-hitting division followed within supporting distance of Heth. Not expecting to encounter any serious resistance, Heth hoped to procure badly needed supplies for his command upon reaching Gettysburg.

This light-hearted air seemed to filter down through the ranks. The column marched along at a leisurely pace. The men chatted and smoked, enjoying the picturesque scenery. After a morning mist, a soft breeze rippled through the ripening grain fields that stretched out from both sides of the Chambersburg Pike.

Meanwhile, on the low ridges west of Gettysburg, elements of Union Brigadier General John Buford's cavalry division lay in wait. It was Buford's 3,000 horsemen, not militia, that Pettigrew had spotted a day earlier. The blue-clad troopers were screening the advance of the left wing of the Army of the Potomac under Major General John F. Reynolds. Buford hoped to prevent the Southerners from occupying Gettysburg and controlling the network of roads that intersected there. Perhaps he could hold on until Reynolds arrived with the vanguard of his infantry.

As Buford's troopers anxiously watched for signs of the enemy, the Union First Corps broke camp at their overnight bivouacs six miles to the south. Unknown to Lee, Meade, and the 2,400 residents of Gettysburg, the leading elements of the two great armies were on a collision course.

13th Alabama
Sergeants Thomas J. Grant & William A. Castleberry, Private William H. Moon, Archer's Brig., Heth's Div., Hill's Corps

The 13th Alabama marched near the front of Heth's column as it advanced toward Gettysburg on July 1. The color-bearer, Sergeant Thomas Grant, "a big double-jointed six-footer" from Wedowa, Alabama, was in fine spirits having imbibed freely of Pennsylvania rye whiskey or hard cider throughout the morning. This devil-may-care attitude received a damper when Colonel Birkett D. Fry rode back to Grant and ordered him to uncase the colors. Private Elijah Boland noted that this act was "the first intimation that we had that we were about to engage the enemy."

As the Southerners neared the low ground in the vicinity of Marsh Creek about three miles from Gettysburg, the first scattering of shots broke the morning stillness. Through the morning fog, the Confederate foot soldiers caught glimpses of shadowy figures on the high ground ahead of them. The column continued its inexorable advance, but the pace was slowed to a crawl due to the harassing fire of the mobile enemy squads, which fell back whenever the Southerners approached to within close range.

Finally, at about 9 a.m., Heth's infantrymen reached Herr Ridge, a partly wooded elevation two miles from the town. Only 1,300 yards to the east, across a stretch of open fields, the general observed the main line of the enemy forming up on a lower rise, known as McPherson's Ridge. In front of the 13th Alabama the dismounted

Battle flag of the 13th Alabama Infantry
Courtesy of Alabama Department of Archives and History

cavalrymen were sheltered by a triangular-shaped woodlot just to the south of a farmhouse owned by Edward McPherson.

Heth deployed his artillery along both sides of the pike and a sharp artillery duel ensued. He then ordered his brigade commanders "to feel the enemy; to make a forced reconnaissance, and determine in what force the enemy were — whether or not he was massing his forces on Gettysburg." Davis' 1,700-man brigade took position on the north side of the road while Archer's 1,200 officers and men filed off to the south directly opposite Herbst's Woods, popularly referred to as "McPherson's Woods."

The 13th Alabama took position near the right of Archer's line near a battery of cannon. After a few minutes, the order "Forward!" rang out. The movement placed the 13th on a direct line between two dueling batteries. The men rushed down the slope toward Willoughby Run, which flowed along the western fringe of the woods. Sergeant Grant waved the flag furiously and hollered at the top of his voice, making himself a conspicuous target for the Union gunners. Private William Moon, a member of the color-guard, turned to his comrade, "Tom, if you don't stop that I will use my bayonet on you." Just then a volley of rifle balls whistled over their heads and Grant needed no further admonition.

Expecting an easy victory, Archer reformed his lines in the sheltered ravine formed by the run. As the regiments clambered up the steep banks and pushed into the woods, they became hotly engaged at close range by onrushing Union infantrymen. These troops, the leading elements of the First Corps, had arrived on the scene just in time to replace Buford's troopers. Archer's Brigade had run headlong into the hard-fighting Iron Brigade.

After firing several volleys, the soldiers of the 13th received orders to fall back. As they returned to the low ground near Willoughby Run, the stunned Alabamians found themselves surrounded by blue coats. As Private Boland expressed it, "[A]ll who had not grasped time by the forelock and left when they realized what a deadly trap we were in surrendered."

Among these unfortunate souls was Private Moon of the color-guard, who would escape from the prison complex at Fort Delaware fifteen months later. Another was General Archer himself who had accompanied his men on foot. Sergeant William Castleberry recalled being directly by Archer's side when the officer was captured. He also claimed to be carrying the colors at this time and made no mention of Grant in his account.

According to Castleberry, Archer plunged his sword into the ground and broke it in half to prevent the trophy from falling into enemy hands. The general also ordered William to drop the flag. The sergeant promptly obeyed, but then recalled the words of his regimental commander: "Don't let the Yankees have them" when he gave him the colors at Chancellorsville. Springing into action, the color-bearer tore the flag from the staff, concealed it around his bosom, and darted for the rear. "As I started off a Yankee struck me with his sword and cursed me, telling me to come back," he recalled, "I told him I would die if I did not get a drink of water soon, for I claimed to be very sick."

Eventually, Castleberry made good on his escape and viewed the next stage of the battle from a patch of timber. Next, he related being discovered by a mounted Confederate officer who asked him what command he belonged to. After receiving the response, the rider galloped away only to return a few moments later. Castleberry was informed that General Lee wished to see him. The nervous enlisted man expected to be placed under guard for straggling. Instead, he was questioned about the fate of General Archer. Lee was very relieved to learn that his brigadier was still alive. At the end of the interrogation, the army chief ordered him to a field hospital that had been established a mile farther to the rear. Before departing Castleberry took the colors from his breast and showed them to his commander. The general rubbed the tears from his eyes and said, "Go on."

55th North Carolina
Colonel John Kerr Connally,
Davis' Brig., Heth's Div., Hill's Corps

Just moments before Archer's Brigade marched into the deadly trap in McPherson's Woods, General Joseph Davis' men confronted Union infantrymen in the ripening grain fields north of the pike. The Confederate battle line advanced steadily up the slope with the 42nd Mississippi on the right, the 2nd Mississippi in the center, and the 55th North Carolina on the left. Because of the undulating nature of the ground, the Tarheels popped into view before the Mississippians and drew the first Union infantry volley of the battle. Two men in the 55th's color-guard fell wounded. The 640 North Carolinians immediately unleashed a devastating return volley. Then Davis' soldiers charged "in magnificent style."

Although the 55th had little combat experience, its commander had already earned a reputation for impetuosity and fierce unit pride. John Kerr Connally, a Yadkin County attorney and former U. S. Naval Academy midshipman served as captain of Company B, 21st North Carolina before being elected as colonel of the 55th on May 19, 1862.

During the spring of 1863 the regiment took part in a siege of a Federal garrison at Suffolk, Virginia.

Colonel John Kerr Connally
North Carolina Office of Archives and History

During a surprise attack one evening a Union squad captured a Confederate artillery piece. In a report of the incident two staff officers from an Alabama brigade erroneously stated that the 55th had been assigned to guard the guns. Outraged by the allegation, Connally immediately sought out the officers and demanded that the report be corrected. Much to his displeasure, the request was denied. After a meeting of the regimental officers, it was decided that Connally and Major Alfred Belo would challenge the Alabamians to a duel, which was accepted.

The next day, the duelists met in a large field near the camp. Major Belo and his opponent chose the Mississippi rifle at forty paces and immediately began the contest. Both men fired two shots and missed with both.

Meanwhile, in another part of the field, the friends of Colonel Connally and his opponent, Captain Leigh Terrell, were engaged in a desperate effort to reach a peaceful settlement of the affair. Tactfully, Terrell admitted his mistake and offered to revise his report. This agreement prevented any hostilities between the two men and came just in time to halt the exchange of a third round of shots by their associates.

Upon making contact with the enemy at Gettysburg, Connally soon realized that his battle line extended far beyond the right flank of the Union position. To maximize this opportunity he ordered the 55th to execute a right wheel. This maneuver would allow his soldiers to fire directly down the length of the Union formation, thus exposing the Yankees to a deadly crossfire.

Several color-bearers of the 55th were shot down during this movement. At this critical juncture, the colonel seized the battle flag and rushed out several paces in front of the regiment. The rash move attracted the fire of the enemy and Connally fell to the ground after sustaining wounds to his left arm and his right hip. Major Belo rushed over to his superior and asked if he was badly wounded. The quick reply was, "Yes, but pay no attention to me! Take the colors and keep ahead of the Mississippians."

As his men rushed after the now fleeing bluecoats, Connally was borne to the rear on a stretcher and later escorted to a field hospital at Cashtown. His close friend, Musician Archibald A. Tyson, volunteered to remain with him after the army returned to Virginia. A Federal surgeon removed the colonel's badly shattered arm shortly after his capture.

Although Connally was released on parole in March 1864 and eventually recovered from his injuries, he was never well enough to resume command of his beloved regiment. Adjutant Charles Cooke wrote that "This was a great loss, for he was not only brave and loyal in his support of the Southern cause, but his sentiments and conduct were so chivalric, that he impressed all the men and officers of the regiment with his own lofty ideals."

Following the war, Connally moved to Texas and practiced criminal law. After relocating to Virginia, he became the youngest man elected to the state senate. When the roof of the state house in Richmond collapsed, several men standing close to him were killed. This close call might have inspired his next career move. Moving back to his native North Carolina, the former lawyer and politician studied for the ministry and developed into an eloquent preacher in Asheville. Shortly before Connally's death in 1904, the United Confederate Veterans awarded him the Cross-of-Honor for his bravery at Gettysburg.

2nd Mississippi
Corporal William B. Murphy,
Davis' Brig., Heth's Div., Hill's Corps

Flushed with victory, Davis' Brigade disintegrated into a "disorganized and yelling mob," and chased the retreating Yankee soldiers towards Gettysburg. Suddenly, a withering volley ripped into the Southerners from across the pike. Seeking refuge from the leaden storm, Davis' men took cover in an unfinished railroad bed that ran roughly parallel and several hundred feet north of the road. Deep cuts existed where the ridges intersected the grading for the depressed bed. The soldiers of the 2nd Mississippi took cover in the deep cut located along the eastern crest of McPherson's Ridge. Scrambling up the steep, rocky bank on the south side, the Confederates peered over the lip of the ledge and beheld a Union regiment lined up behind a post and rail fence one hundred and seventy five paces away.

Led by Lieutenant Colonel Rufus Dawes, the black-hatted soldiers of the 6th Wisconsin were familiar opponents to the men of the 2nd Mississippi. Less than ten months earlier, the two units took part in the bloody struggle for the cornfield near the Dunker Church at the Battle of Antietam, or Sharpsburg, and both had suffered horrific losses.

As the Mississippi officers struggled to organize their jumbled commands in the narrow confines of the cut, the infantrymen peppered away at the exposed Northerners. Suddenly, with a throaty yell, the Wisconsin soldiers clambered over the fence and surged to-

Battle flag of the 2nd Mississippi Infantry captured by the 6th Wisconsin at the Railroad Cut on July 1, 1863. Corporal William Murphy was taken prisoner while serving as color bearer.

Courtesy of Old Capitol Museum
Mississippi Department of Archives and History

wards the Mississippians. As Dawes' men sprinted through the open field on the opposite side of the road they spied a Rebel color waving defiantly above the edge of the railroad cut. "A heroic ambition to capture it took possession of several of our men," recalled the Wisconsin colonel. As the Yankees closed in on the prize, they could read the battle honors of the veteran 2nd Mississippi painted in yellow-gold in Gothic style letters on each quadrant of the cross: "Seven Pines," "Manassas," "Gaines Farm," and "Malvern Hill." The flag staff had been thrust deeply into the ground in the grassy meadow "about fifty paces East of the cut, and on the side towards Gettysburg...about ten paces South of the railroad."

Surrounded by his escort, Corporal William B. Murphy tightly clutched the wooden staff of the standard as the attack swept towards him. A member of the color guard since April 1861, Murphy had carried the colors through all of the actions emblazoned upon the regimental banner. However, he was not slated for the post of honor on July 1. The 2nd's color sergeant, Christopher Columbus Davis, was sick on the opening day of the battle. Thus, William assumed his familiar role and stood in the center of the deadly storm where to one Wisconsin soldier "it seemed almost impossible to breathe without inhaling a bullet." Murphy later wrote:

> My color guards were all killed and wounded in less than five minutes, and also my colors were shot more than one dozen times, and the flag staff was hit and splintered two or three times. Just about that time a squad of soldiers made a rush for my colors.... They were all killed or wounded, but they still rushed for the colors with one of the most deadly struggles that was ever witnessed during any battle in the war. They still kept rushing for my flag and there were over a dozen shot down like sheep....

Two incidents testify to the savage nature of the struggle for the colors. Corporal Lewis Eggleston of Company H was among the first group of soldiers from the 6th to reach Murphy. As young Lewis and a comrade grasped the staff of the Confederate flag a Mississippi corporal fired at them from his knees at point blank range. Both men were wounded by the blast, Eggleston mortally. In retaliation, Private James "Rocky Mountain" Anderson clubbed his musket and with a forceful blow split the skull of the shooter.

Private John Harland of Company I was also shot just as he reached for the flag, his body tumbling into the railroad cut at the foot of the soldier who had killed him. Enraged by the slaying of his friend, Levi Tongue drew a bead on the offender. In response to the Confederate's desperate plea, "Don't shoot! Don't kill me!" Tongue responded, "All hell can't save you now." He yanked the trigger and his adversary fell backward onto Harland's body.

Finally, a contingent of Wisconsin soldiers sealed off the shallow eastern end of the cut while others stood at the brow and pointed their muskets down at Davis' ensnared soldiers. After a few tense moments, surrender was negotiated between Dawes and Major John A. Blair of the 2nd Mississippi.

Meanwhile, the all-consuming struggle for Murphy's flag raged on, the impassioned combatants seemingly oblivious to anything but the chain of events unfolding within their tiny corner of the universe. Through the twisted tangle of wounded and dying soldiers, 22-year-old Union Corporal Francis Wallar, a robust man, "who never missed a battle or a meal," closed in on Murphy. Wallar later admitted that he had no thought of going for the flag until the opportunity suddenly presented itself. As he lunged toward the elusive prize, a Confederate pointed his weapon at Francis, but his brother Sam, who advanced by his side, knocked the gun barrel away just as it discharged. In desperation, Corporal Murphy began to tear the flag from the staff. At this climactic moment Wallar took hold of the gallant standard-bearer and wrenched the colors away, an act that would later earn him a Medal of Honor.

After a brief moment of indecision, Wallar stood upon the captured banner and fired two shots at the enemy. Shortly afterward, he turned the trophy over to his commander. Dawes tore the flag from the staff and tied it around the body of Sergeant William Evans, who having been shot through both legs was hobbling to the rear using two muskets as crutches. Along with several other members of his unit, the wounded sergeant eventually gained refuge inside the home of Jacob Hollinger on York Street. Later in the day, as the Confederates surged into the town, Evans begged his comrades to hide the flag. Thinking quickly, the soldiers sliced a hole in the bed-tick beneath Evans and stuffed the banner inside the compartment.

As the Wisconsin sergeant staggered into town with his strange new undergarment, Murphy and over 200 fellow prisoners were escorted to Cemetery Hill. After dark, the sullen captives commenced a long march to West Chester, Pennsylvania. Near the beginning of the trek, the Southern color bearer suffered still another indignity. After refusing to give up an expensive pair of field glasses, a member of the guard punched him in the side and took them away. This "cowardly act" capped an already distressing day for Murphy.

When later asked why his color guard did not protect him, William replied, "They did all that mortal men could do in the defense of the flag, as they all lost their lives in the defense of their country." Lieutenant Colonel Dawes agreed. In reference to the color-party of the 2nd Mississippi, he wrote, "They have no cause to blush, or we to exalt."

Murphy arrived at Fort Delaware Prison on July 6. Three weeks later, he escaped and reached his regiment by mid-August. Awarded a furlough, the sergeant returned to his home in northern Mississippi. But his misfortune continued when a Union cavalry patrol scooped him up. Murphy was eventually shuttled back to Delaware, where he remained incarcerated until June 13, 1865.

After the war, Murphy and Dawes exchanged a series of friendly letters concerning the central event in both of their lives. In 1892, the ex-Confederate wrote his former adversary, "I would like very much to have my old flag back again for a keep sake; there is nothing that I would appreciate more highly than to see it once more in my life as I am 50 years in July 13, 1892.... Oh, it seems as if it were only yesterday since that deadly conflict in the Railroad Cut at Gettysburg."

Four years later, Murphy visited the battlefield and stood upon the exact spot where the fierce struggle for the colors took place. The old Rebel had no regrets, but he conceded that the outcome of the war was a "blessing for the American people...for now we are all one and live under the best government in the world." Murphy's flag was returned to the state of Mississippi in 1905 by order of the United States War Department.

By 11 a.m., the opening round of the first day's battle had ended. The results were not encouraging for the Southerners. Two of Heth's brigades had been badly mauled and driven back. But plenty of daylight remained as both armies rushed reinforcements to the scene. During the midday lull, the remainder of the Union First Corps arrived and was soon joined by Major General Oliver O. Howard's

Eleventh Corps. The First Corps, led by Major General Abner Doubleday, was positioned to block the western approaches to the town while Howard posted his men on the open plain north of Gettysburg. During the early morning, Robert E. Lee rode eastward on the Chambersburg Pike toward the sound of the firing. Heth was eager to resume the fighting, but Lee, reluctant to further escalate the affair until Longstreet's veterans arrived, reined him in. However, events would continue to spiral out of his control.

Receiving word from A. P. Hill that elements of the Third Corps were advancing upon Gettysburg, Richard Ewell led his troops toward the town to support his fellow corps commander. Rodes' Division marched south down the Carlisle Road as Early's Division approached the field from the northeast via the Harrisburg Road. The battle was building toward an even bloodier stage.

5th Alabama
Private George Nutting,
O'Neal's Brig., Rodes' Div., Ewell's Corps

As Rodes' Division approached the town the sweating infantrymen filed off the road to the right and advanced across an oak-covered eminence. The increasing heat and humidity exacted a severe physical toll on the soldiers. "I was perfectly exhausted & never suffered so from heat & fatigue in my life," wrote Corporal Samuel Pickens, 5th Alabama, one of the regiments that formed Colonel Edward O'Neal's Brigade.

Pickens' friend and messmate, Private George "Tone" Nutting of Greensboro, Alabama, was the regimental color-bearer. The two men had enlisted in Company D, the "Greensboro Guards," during the previous year. Although perhaps as many as eighty soldiers dropped out from heat exhaustion during the movement, Pickens and Nutting persevered.

Upon reaching Oak Hill, Generals Ewell and Rodes viewed the battle line of the First Corps spread out below them. Excited by the prospect of striking a crippling blow, Ewell ordered Rodes to attack. O'Neal's Alabama soldiers took position on the wooded eastern slope of the hill as Brigadier General Alfred Iverson's North Carolinians assembled near the present location of the Eternal Light Peace Memorial. Brigadier General Junius Daniel formed his men to the right rear of Iverson and Brigadier General Stephen Ramseur's brigade occupied the support line.

In their eagerness to attack the Southern officers failed to properly reconnoiter the enemy position. As Rodes' prepared his assault, Doubleday shuffled troops from his reserve force to Oak Ridge, just below the summit of the hill, to counter the threat to his exposed flank.

The 5th Alabama was originally held in reserve but joined the latter stages of the doomed attack. As the regiment rushed down the farm lane of the Moses McClean farm, it was subjected to volleys from the front and blasted by musketry and artillery fire from the left. Caught in a deadly cross-fire, the entire brigade fell back in confusion in an action that lasted only about fifteen minutes.

In the short but spirited encounter, Company D suffered the loss of one killed, five wounded, and three captured. The lone mortality devastated the tightly knit Greensboro Guards. As the attack ground to a halt, Color bearer Nutting shouted "Come on boys!" to encourage his faltering comrades. Shot down almost immediately, he died on the field moments later.

Modern view of the Moses McClean farm. Private George Nutting, 5th Alabama, received a mortal wound in this vicinity.

Corporal Pickens, who had left the field to assist a wounded comrade, received the sad news later in the day. He recorded in his diary that his friend died with the colors and that "a nobler, more generous boy never lived. He was a great favorite & will be much missed." A few days later, a grief-stricken Lieutenant E. P. Jones wrote to his sister:

> Our loss was not heavy compared to what the loss was in some other companies of the regiment; but still we feel deeply and mourn much the death of poor "Tone." I know of no one in the company who would have been missed more and talked of as much as he, in fact, he was the life of the company, always in a good humor, full of fun and as brave as a lion. Every one in the company liked him, and feel that we have not only lost a brave soldier, but a friend whose place cannot be filled.

20th North Carolina
Lieutenant John D. Irvin
Iverson's Brig., Rodes' Div., Ewell's Corps

While O'Neal's attack bogged down on the opposite side of the hill, Iverson's four regiments, numbering about 1,400 men, emerged from a patch of woods near the Mummasburg Road and entered a large grassy field. As the North Carolinians descended the gradual slope, the battle line veered to the left towards a low stone wall that bordered the eastern edge of the meadow. A Southern officer remembered that the brigade marched "in gallant style, as evenly as if on parade."

Behind the wall, an equal number of Union soldiers waited as Iverson's troops "came sweeping on in magnificent order, with perfect alignment, guns at right shoulder and colors to the front — to many a dead march." When the Confederates reached a low swale about fifty yards from the wall, the concealed enemy riflemen delivered a well-aimed volley. The gray formation instantly evaporated as hundreds of men tumbled to the ground side by side.

Unable to advance or retreat through the deadly fusillade, the surviving Tarheels hugged the ground hoping that fate would spare them from the deadly missiles flying at them seemingly from every direction. "I believe every man who stood up was either killed or wounded," wrote one officer. Indeed, during the brief action Iverson lost about 900 men, the highest percentage loss suffered by a Confederate brigade at Gettysburg.

In light of these staggering casualties, First Lieutenant John D. Irvin seemed fortunate to lose only a finger from his left hand. The Cabarras County native earned a living as a carpenter before enlisting as a private in Company A of the 20th North Carolina at age 22 on May 23, 1861. He advanced steadily in rank, reaching his current grade in September 1862.

After the color party of the 20th was decimated on the bloody afternoon of July 1, Lt. Irvin took possession of the standard. By this stage, a number of his desperate comrades had raised tokens of surrender, including boots and hats hoisted upon bayonets. Suddenly, screaming blue infantrymen charged over the wall toward Iverson's shell-shocked soldiers. Gripped by inertia, the Southerners could not decide upon the best course of action — to lie still, surrender, or fight to the death.

Opportunistic Yankees singled out the hapless color bearers. Sergeant Sylvester Riley of the 97th New York seized the colors of the 20th North Carolina from Lieutenant Irvin and then immediately handed them to Lieutenant Ebenezer Harrington. After the 97th returned to its former position, Harrington presented the captured standard to Colonel Charles Wheelock, the regimental commander. The colonel waved the flag triumphantly as his men resumed their places in the brigade line.

Spotting the red banner fluttering along the wall, General Henry Baxter dispatched an order directing that the flag be sent to the rear. Wheelock refused, declaring that "my regiment captured these colors and will keep them." With the assistance of one of his junior officers the New Yorker cut the flag from the wooden staff with his sword and then sliced the fabric in half.

Later in the day, as Union forces retreated through the town, Captain Alexander H. Gallaway of the 45th North Carolina recaptured one of the halves of the 20th's regimental flag. Reportedly, it contained twenty-seven bullet holes.

Lieutenant John Irvin's military career was far from over after Gettysburg. Wounded in the right leg during the Overland Campaign in the spring of 1864, he returned to duty in September only to be captured at the battle of Third Winchester on the 19th. The officer remained a prisoner of war until his release on June 14, 1865.

In 1913, thousands of Union and Confederate veterans assembled in Gettysburg to celebrate the fiftieth anniversary of the great battle. Near the beginning of the reunion, Henry Fitzgerald, a former sergeant in the 97th New York walked into the camp of the North Carolina veterans and asked if he could speak to any surviving member of the 20th North Carolina. Immediately, someone shoved John Irvin to the front stating, "He's the color bearer of the Twentieth."

"The color bearer!" exclaimed an overjoyed Fitzgerald. "That's better than I hoped for. I've got the other half of your flag that we took away from you fifty years ago today, and I wanted to return it to somebody from that regiment, but I didn't hope to be able to give it to the very man we took it from."

The former combatants then sat down together and reminisced about the unforgettable events in which they had participated a half-century ago.

At about 2:30 p.m., Henry Heth received permission to renew his attack on McPherson's Ridge. With Ewell's troops arriving from the north, there appeared to be an excellent opportunity to crush the Federal forces. General Pettigrew's 2,500 men would spearhead Heth's new attack. The daunting task of clearing out McPherson's Woods fell to the 26th North Carolina.

26th North Carolina

Colonel Henry King Burgwyn, Jr.,
Lt. Col. John R. Lane, Sgt. Jefferson Mansfield,
& Pvt. John Vinson
Pettigrew's Brig., Heth's Div., Hill's Corps

The order to attack greatly relieved Colonel Henry Burgwyn, Jr. Valuable daylight was slipping away and with it the opportunity for battlefield glory. Throughout the morning and early afternoon, harassing sniper fire and stray artillery shells reminded the men of the dangerous work that lay ahead. Indeed, the only thing worse than combat itself was waiting to go into action.

Suddenly, the long anticipated command, "Attention!" rang out along the line. Over 800 strong, the officers and men of the 26th

North Carolina hustled to their assigned places. Colonel Burgwyn posted himself directly behind the center of the regiment. Accompanied by his eight-man color guard, Sergeant Jefferson Mansfield stepped four paces in front of the formation. The 25-year-old sergeant had left behind two young sons and a wife whom he loved deeply. In his last letter home he informed her that he expected "hard fighting before we get back. We must put our trust in God."

Upon the order to "Forward, March!" the 26th stepped off and "made as pretty and perfect a line as a regiment ever made every man endeavoring to keep dressed on the colors." As they advanced down the open slope of Herr Ridge, enemy volleys exploded from the edge of the timberline. An ankle wound knocked Sergeant Mansfield out of the action. Sergeant Hiram Johnson immediately took possession of the colors, but he, too, was hit and the flag passed to Private John Stamper of Company A. This pattern would be repeated with alarming frequency during the next half-hour. "Although they knew it was almost certain death to pick it up, the flag was never allowed to remain down, but as fast as it fell some one raised it again," recalled an enlisted man.

Lt. Colonel John R. Lane (left), Colonel Henry K. Bergwyn, Jr. (center), and Zebulon B. Vance, the original colonel of the 26th North Carolina.

Courtesy of the North Carolina Office of Archives and History

Bursting with pride, the boy colonel rode along the line and with his clear and commanding voice cheered the men onward. When the 26th reached the ravine along Willoughby Run the thick underbrush disrupted their perfect alignment. Artillery shells raked the right flank of the line as bullets "thick as hail stones in a storm" pummeled the formation from the front. Carrying the standard near the stream, Pvt. Stamper was hit in the right shoulder by one of the missiles. Private George Washington Kelly replaced Stamper but a bullet struck him in the ankle as he leapt to the opposite bank. Kelly's friend, Private Larkin Thomas, then took charge of the colors.

Once his troops cleared the steep banks of the stream, Burgwyn reformed his line for another assault against the 24th Michigan of the Iron Brigade, which had fallen back to a more sheltered location in the woods. Soon after the advance resumed, Thomas received a wound to his left arm and he passed the banner to Private John Vinson. This Company G member was an unlikely candidate for this post of honor. A court martial had found Vinson guilty of deserting the army back in March and had sentenced him to death by a firing squad. Released from arrest to participate in the battle, he quickly redeemed his honor by being wounded in action with the colors. The next flag bearer, 19-year-old Private John Marley, fell dead with the staff in his hands.

By the time the Tarheels pushed the stubborn defenders out of the grove, the flag had been cut down ten times and every member of the color guard was out of the action. Captain William W. McCreery, an officer serving on Pettigrew's staff, rushed forward to Burgwyn with a message from the general that the 26th had "covered itself with glory today." It was the crowning moment of accomplishment for the ambitious young officer, but the elation proved short-lived.

A new Federal battle line, the 467 officers and men of the 151st Pennsylvania, suddenly materialized in the southeast corner of the woodlot. The two lines closed to within twenty paces and exchanged devastating volleys. Inspired by the courage of the 26th's soldiery, Captain McCreery lifted the regimental colors from a dead color-bearer and proudly waved them aloft. Within seconds, a bullet entered his heart and the officer pitched forward, drenching the banner with his blood. Lieutenant George Wilcox pulled the blood-soaked standard from underneath McCreery's lifeless form and pushed ahead into the maelstrom. After a few steps, two rounds pierced his chest, but he survived.

Fearing that his troops might falter at this critical juncture, Burgwyn seized the flag staff from Wilcox. With his outstretched sword in one hand and the flag in the other, he ordered the regiment to "Dress on the colors!" As the survivors rallied around their regimental symbol, Private Frank Honeycutt of Company B rushed up to his commander's side and asked to carry the flag. As Burgwyn turned to hand it over, a bullet slammed into his side. The impact of the blow spun him around, the folds of the flag wrapping around his body as he collapsed to the earth. An instant later, a bullet thudded into Honeycutt's head.

Lieutenant Colonel John R. Lane rushed over to Burgwyn. "My dear colonel, are you severely hurt?" he asked. Henry replied by weakly squeezing the hand of the 27-year-old officer as he gestured toward the gaping wound in his side. Lane recalled that Burgwyn looked "as pleasantly as if victory was on his brow." Reluctantly, he departed to take charge of the regiment.

Lane picked up the downed flag and led the regiment forward once again. A nearby lieutenant protested, "No man can take those colors and live!" Lane replied, "It is my time to take them now! Forward the 26th." General Pettigrew reportedly stated that it was the bravest act that he had ever witnessed. As the final enemy line gave way Lane turned his head to check on the progress of the troops. Just then a bullet crashed through his neck, jaw, and mouth, making him the fourteenth member of the 26th North Carolina to be either killed or wounded with the colors on July 1. One nearby soldier recalled that the officer "fell as limber as a rag." Miraculously, Lane survived these ghastly injuries as well as three subsequent wounds during the final two years of the war.

Burgwyn was not as fortunate. As the 26th swept toward victory, Private William Cheek, Company E, and two other soldiers carried the severely wounded officer off the field. At one point Henry asked the men to set him down in order to pour water over his burning wound. Soon afterward, the trio departed to search for a stretcher.

By the time they returned the young colonel was sinking fast. He lingered for about two hours after his wounding before quietly passing away in the arms of his close friend, Lieutenant Louis G. Young. After sending his love to his family, Burgwyn uttered his final words, "I know my gallant regiment will do their duty — where is my sword?" Private Cheek recalled him saying: "The Lord's will be done. We have gained the greatest victory in the war. I have no regret at my approaching death. I fell in the defense of my country." Still another witness quoted the colonel's farewell as, "Tell the General my men never failed me at a single point."

No matter what he said, Burgwyn, like his old mentor, Stonewall Jackson, immediately became a hero martyr for the South. These sentiments were perhaps best expressed by Captain Joseph J. Young, who wrote, "The death of one so young, so brave, so accomplished, with every prospect of being at no distant period one of our greatest men, has filled all with sadness and sorrow.... I have lost one of my best friends. I can truly say, the death of General Lee himself I would have preferred."

Henry was buried under a walnut tree near a farmhouse along the Chambersburg Pike in a crude coffin fashioned from a gun case. In the spring of 1867 his remains were exhumed and placed in Oakwood Cemetery in Raleigh, North Carolina. His family had the following words inscribed upon his tombstone: "The Lord Gave, and the Lord Hath Taken Away." These words also rang true for the 26th. Only 216 out of the 800 members of the regiment emerged unscathed from the horrific fighting on July 1, 1863.

Private Vinson received his death sentence a year later. Wounded at the Battle of the Wilderness on May 5, 1864, his shattered right leg was amputated. He died three months later in a Lynchburg, Virginia, hospital. Sergeant Mansfield returned home to father many more children.

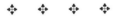

Exhausted and nearly out of ammunition, Pettigrew's men did not pursue the retiring Union regiments toward Seminary Ridge. Fortunately for the Southerners, help was on the way. William Dorsey Pender's "Light Division" was marching to the scene. These veteran soldiers had earned a reputation as some of the best shock troops in Lee's army. They seemed to have a knack for arriving on the field at the most opportune moment and then delivering a knockout blow to the opposition.

Pender ordered his men to pass through Heth's shattered division and charge the reforming Federal line. Several hundred yards to the east on a parallel ridge, Pender's men spotted the four-story brick dormitory and classroom of the Lutheran Theological Seminary.

Along the outer edge of a wooded grove just west of the building, the decimated regiments of the Union First Corps hunkered behind a breastwork of earth and fence rails. Even more menacing, nearly two dozen artillery pieces crowned the ridge. Through the thick canopy of trees ahead of them the attackers caught glimpses of the town and of the prominent heights of Cemetery Hill just beyond. The grandeur of the scene soon faded into the tumult of battle.

13th North Carolina
Sergeant William F. Faucette &
Pvt. Levi J. Walker
Scales' Brig., Pender's Div., Hill's Corps

The 1,400 North Carolinians of General Alfred Scales' Brigade advanced directly into the teeth of the deadly cannon. The gradually sloping, open ground presented the First Corps artillerists with "the fairest field and finest front for destruction on an advancing foe that could well be conceived." A Union soldier recalled that the batteries on the ridge "blazed with a solid sheet of flame, and the missiles of death that swept its western slopes no human being could endure. After a few moments of the belching of the artillery, the blinding smoke shut out the sun and obstructed the view." When the smoke lifted, "Only the dead and dying remained on the bloody slopes of Seminary Ridge."

Within a few moments, Scales' Brigade was virtually annihilated. Only about 500 of the Tarheels escaped death or injury and these survivors lay pinned down less than a hundred yards from the Union position. The casualties in the 13th North Carolina, in particular, were staggering. From a battle strength of 232 officers and men, the unit suffered 55 killed, 98 wounded, and 26 missing or captured, a nearly 80% loss rate. At least five color bearers were shot down during the deadly assault. In his reminiscences of the war, Confederate General John B. Gordon described a colorful vignette involving one of these men:

> At Big Falls, North Carolina, there lived in 1897 a one-armed soldier whose heroism will be cited by orators and poets as long as heroism is cherished by men. He was a color-bearer of his regiment, the Thirteenth North Carolina. In a charge during the first

day's battle at Gettysburg, his right arm, with which he bore the colors, was shivered and almost torn from its socket. Without halting or hesitating, he seized the falling flag in his left hand, and, with his blood spouting from the severed arteries and his right arm dangling in shreds at his side, he still rushed to the front, shouting to his comrades: "Forward, forward!" The name of that modest and gallant soldier is W. F. Faucette.

A gifted and talented writer, Gordon was well known for his flowery and often embellished accounts. In this instance, the story is largely factual. William Franklin Faucette, a 28-year-old saddler from Alamance County, enlisted as a private in Company E of the 13th North Carolina on May 3, 1861. He was promoted to corporal on May 3, 1863, and then to color sergeant on June 27, just four days before the Battle of Gettysburg. Sergeant Faucette did indeed suffer a compound fracture on July 1, but the injury was sustained to his left arm, not the right as Gordon stated in his narrative. The missile struck the sergeant on the outer elbow and passed through the inner side of the joint.

Captured on July 5, Faucette was admitted to the U. S. General Hospital in Chester, Pennsylvania, two weeks later. His shattered left arm was amputated on September 22. After his condition improved, he was transferred to Point Lookout, Maryland, and then released through an exchange on March 17, 1864. After an examination at Chimborazo Hospital in Richmond, Virginia, he received a furlough and was discharged in the fall.

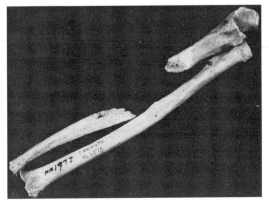

The amputated left arm bone of Sgt. William F. Faucette, 13th North Carolina.

. Anatomical Collections, National Museum of Health and Medicine, Armed Forces Institute of Pathology, Washington, D.C.

William married Phoebe Catherine Blanchard in the spring of 1867. The couple operated a small farm near Big Falls, North Carolina (population 66 in 1895), where they raised eight children. William died of a heart attack at a corn shucking on November 14, 1902.

The identities of the next three men to advance the colors of the 13th North Carolina during the assault on Seminary Ridge are not known. The fifth individual to grasp the standard was 21-year-old Private Levi Jasper Walker of Company B. Levi and his older brother, Henry, enlisted in the "Ranaleburg Riflemen" on May 20, 1861. Raised on a farm in Mecklenburg County, Levi worked as a farmer and textile worker before the war while his older sibling earned a living by teaching. Henry rose to the rank of lieutenant by the spring of 1863, but Levi spent his entire service time as a private.

Carrying the regimental colors on July 1, Private Walker fell with a wound in his left leg. At a nearby field hospital a surgeon removed the damaged limb just below the knee joint. Later captured by Federal forces, Levi was confined at a prison hospital at Davids Island in New York Harbor, until paroled and exchanged in October.

Lieutenant Henry Walker emerged from the fierce fighting unscathed, but twelve days later during a skirmish near Hagerstown, Maryland, he, too, was wounded in the left leg. His injury also required amputation, and remarkably, his limb was removed at nearly the exact location as his brother's at Gettysburg. Like his brother, he was also picked up by Union troops, remaining a prisoner at Johnson's Island, a detention facility for Confederate officers, until May 1864.

In a letter home written on July 20, 1863, a soldier from the 13th confirmed that the Walker brothers "both had their left legs broken and cut off. They were cut off just below the knee."

Neither man allowed his handicap to hold him back after the war, as the brothers became honored citizens of Charlotte, North Carolina. Ironically, Henry studied medicine, afterwards establishing a thriving practice and opening two drugstores. Levi retired as a successful merchant. For one of the brothers, their remarkably similar war injuries turned out to be a blessing. A mutual friend related a remarkable incident that took place on Levi's wedding day:

> The day for the wedding was set and all preparations made. But on that eventful day, and only a few hours before the ceremony was to take place, the prospective bridegroom met with an accident

which seemed like the unfriendly dealing of fate. He slipped and in some way broke his cork leg. Deprived of this very useful member, the young man found that he could not possibly "stand up" for the ceremony, and was therefore in quite a dilemma. At this important juncture, his brother, Dr. H. J. Walker, went forward and saved the day by offering to loan his leg to his brother. The proffered leg was gladly accepted and found to fit perfectly. This is perhaps the only case on record in which one man has been married while standing on the leg of another.

(Left) The Walker brothers at the time of their enlistment in April 1861.
(Right) The brothers circa 1880, replicating their military pose.
Levi appears on the left in both images.

Courtesy of the North Carolina Office of Archives and History

14th South Carolina
Sergeant T. Rutledge Owens
Perrin's Brig., Pender's Div., Hill's Corps

Meanwhile, Colonel Abner Perrin's Brigade of 1,600 South Carolina troops advanced toward the breastworks near the Seminary. As the Southerners approached a fence several hundred yards from the grove, the brigade was exposed to a lethal volley of musketry from the sheltered Union infantrymen. The line wavered under the murderous fire, but the officers realized that "To stop was destruction. To retreat was disaster. To go forward was orders." As Lt. Colonel Joseph N. Brown and the 14th South Carolina pushed forward, the breastworks suddenly erupted into "a sheet of fire and smoke, sending its leaden missiles of death in the faces of men who had often, but never so terribly, met it before." At the same time, the Union artillerists began to train their sights on Perrin's Brigade after decimating Scales' command.

The dead, the wounded, and the dying soldiers of the 14th pitched to the ground with every step. Within a few minutes Sergeant T. Rutledge Owens and his entire color guard but one were slain. Rutledge was the son of Captain Robert S. Owens, who fell at Frazier's Farm a year earlier.

Peering through the thick smoke from his position just north of the Seminary, Lieutenant James A. Gardner, an officer serving in James Cooper's Battery B, 1st Pennsylvania Artillery, watched as the combined fire of the infantry and artillery "staggered and checked Perrin and almost annihilated the left of his brigade." In the heat of battle, Gardner marveled at the bravery of a single color-bearer, the only man to reach the rail barricade. Apparently, Colonel Charles Wainwright, the First Corps artillery chief, observed the same individual as he recalled that "a big fellow had planted the colours of his regiment on a pile of rails within fifty yards of the muzzles of Cooper's guns...." This individual is thought to have been the last surviving member of the 14th's color guard on July 1.

Lieutenant Colonel Brown later memorialized the men who perished during the assault. His words are certainly applicable to the unknown members of the color party that performed their duties under the most trying of circumstances:

Hundreds of brave men fell, most of them young, and on the threshold of life, whose names were not recorded in the official reports of the battle. But they still live in the memories of the loved ones at home, and years afterwards their bodies were removed to Southern cemeteries by patriotic and loving hands. Here let them rest until the morning of the resurrection.

1st South Carolina
Corporal Albert Owens & Cpl. James Larkin
Perrin's Brig., Pender's Div., Hill's Corps

Realizing that the position could not be carried by a frontal assault, Colonel Perrin directed the 1st South Carolina to maneuver to the right and swing around into the rear of the enemy lines. The order was brilliantly executed and the defenders collapsed like a row of dominos. But the victory did not come without cost. Before retreating in confusion towards Gettysburg, the Union infantrymen holding the left flank of the line unloosed an well-aimed volley at the onrushing Southerners. The South Carolinians wavered for a moment.

Apparently, the 1st South Carolina carried two stands of colors that day. Corporal Albert P. Owens of Company E and Corporal James Larkin, Company H, rushed to the front waving their flags and yelled for the regiment to "come on." Soon afterwards, Larkin collapsed after bullets ripped through his right shoulder and lungs. Owens rushed over and picked up Larkin's downed flag then led the advance with both colors. An instant later, a minie ball smashed into his right thigh, badly shattering the bone. Captain Washington Shooter wrote that Owens had "behaved gloriously" but feared that his wound was of a mortal nature.

When the Union lines broke the jubilant Southerners surged past the Seminary close on the heels of their adversaries. The disorganized mob of Yankees descended the steep eastern slope of Seminary Ridge and then picked their way through the labyrinth of streets and alleys toward Cemetery Hill. "Now the Rebel turn came to kill," noted one Southern officer with obvious satisfaction. The Confederates also gathered up a large number of blue-clad soldiers and captured several stands of colors.

The 1st South Carolina became the first Southern regiment to enter Gettysburg and its proud members hoisted their banner upon the flagpole at the center of the square. General Pender galloped up to the regiment and upon the sight of the colors, he was inspired to doff his hat. The general paid the men of the 1st his highest compliments and stated that they had done enough for one day. He ordered the troops to go to the rear for rest and water.

Both Larkin and Owens were left behind in area field hospitals when the army withdrew from Pennsylvania. The pair was transported to De Camp General Hospital at Davids Island, NY. Confirming Captain Shooter's grim prognosis, Corporal Owens passed away there on August 6. Later that month, Larkin received a parole and passed back into friendly lines. Due to health complications, he checked into Chimborazo Hospital on Christmas Eve. His fighting days over, Larkin would spend much of 1864 serving in the Invalid Corps, an organization made up of disabled soldiers that performed garrison duty and other non-combat functions.

On February 17, 1864, the Confederate Congress authorized a commissioned officer known as an ensign to carry the colors. He held the rank of a first lieutenant but had no command authority. Although Corporal Larkin was considered permanently disabled for field service, Captain Shooter recommended that he be considered for an honorary promotion to this grade, writing:

> He always proved himself a good soldier in camp and a brave one on the field. For many months past, he has been color-bearer and acted in that capacity at Fredericksburg, Chancellorsville, and Gettysburg. In all of these battles, he bore himself with conspicuous gallantry; at Gettysburg, where he received the wound which disabled him, he was leading the regiment under a hot fire. He is a native of Baltimore and without friends or kindred in the Confederacy.

The recommendation was approved and Larkin ascended to the rank of ensign on April 23, 1864. Seven months later, he received a full military discharge.

As Pender's men broke through the Federal lines near the Seminary, Robert Rodes continued to apply pressure against the stubborn Union defenders on Oak Ridge. After a series of disjointed attacks, the Confederates finally managed to utilize their superior numbers in this sector. As General Junius Daniel's Brigade swept through the fields north of the unfinished railroad, Brigadier General Stephen Dodson Ramseur's four North Carolina regiments struck the apex of the Union position along the Mummasburg Road. Ramseur massed his firepower against the unprotected right flank of the Union line. O'Neal's Alabama troops and the remnants of Iverson's shattered brigade joined the assault. Outgunned and running low on ammunition, the blue coats fell back along the ridge.

14th North Carolina
Sergeant Bennett Russell
Ramseur's Brig., Rodes' Div., Ewell's Corps

MAP REF. 10

Seeking protection from the converging Confederate forces many of the retreating Yankee soldiers fled toward the town along the unfinished railroad bed. With great satisfaction General Ramseur noted that the enemy "ran off the field in confusion, leaving his killed and wounded and between 800 and 900 prisoners in our hands." A member of Ramseur's 14th North Carolina recalled that he could "hear their bones crunch under the shot and shell." Conversely, the attackers suffered comparatively minor losses. For instance, the 300-man 14th North Carolina lost only about one-fifth of its strength on July 1.

Unlike many of his fellow color-bearers, Sergeant Bennett Russell emerged from the battle without a scratch. Two years earlier, the 28-year-old Stanly County farmer enlisted as a private in Company H of the 14th North Carolina. By the close of 1862 he had been promoted to sergeant. After suffering a head wound at Chancellorsville, he was back in the ranks when the army marched toward Pennsylvania in June.

By all accounts Russell would never have been mistaken for Rhett Butler. A comrade described him as "illiterate, unassuming in manners, plain and not prepossessing in appearance." He did, however, concede that the color sergeant was "noble, generous, and brave." In describing an incident that took place in Chambersburg, Pa., a week before the battle, another soldier from the 14th was even less flattering:

> Bennett Russell was our color sergeant. A brave, good soldier
> —but plain, homely (well if you must have it), "ugly as home-made
> sin." A woman standing by the roadside, seeing our uniforms were
> worn, dirty and ragged, asked Bennett why we did not wear better

clothes? Bennett replied, "We always put on our old clothes in which to kill hogs" (Yankees). He told her she was the finest-looking and the puttiest "gal" he "had ever saw" and asked her for a kiss, which she indignantly refused. Bennett and this girl were two of the ugliest mortals the writer ever saw.

But what Russell lacked in looks he made up for in good fortune. Not only did he survive Gettysburg; he subsequently carried the colors through some of the bloodiest battles of the war until he was paroled at Appomattox Court House on April 9, 1865.

As the divisions of Pender and Rodes finally dislodged the stubborn defenders of the Union First Corps from the low ridges west of town, another decisive action was taking place north of Gettysburg. During the early afternoon, two divisions of Major General Oliver O. Howard's Eleventh Corps deployed across an open valley below Oak Ridge. On the far right, General Francis Barlow pushed his troops beyond the original line to seize the only high ground in the area, a sparsely wooded knoll that overlooked Rock Creek near the Harrisburg Road. The Union brigade positioned on Blocher's Knoll had borne the brunt of Stonewall Jackson's flank attack at Chancellorsville only two months earlier. They were about to suffer a similar fate at Gettysburg.

While Barlow took position on the northeast outskirts of town, General Jubal Early's Division marched down the Harrisburg Road towards the sound of heavy firing. Early's fortuitous arrival spelled disaster for the unlucky Eleventh Corps. Observing that the Northern troops ahead of him were isolated and poorly posted, "Old Jube" formed a line of battle across both sides of the road and prepared to strike. The brunt of the assault fell to five Georgia regiments from Brigadier General John B. Gordon's Brigade.

31st Georgia
Private David Raiford Adams
Gordon's Brig., Early's Div., Ewell's Corps

A 31-year-old former lawyer with no military background, John B. Gordon entered Confederate service as a captain, but through his gallantry and ambition he quickly rose through the ranks. A born leader and powerful orator, the general served as an inspiring example to his troops and they reciprocated with unflinching loyalty. Always leading from the front, he survived several close calls during the first two years of the war, including ghastly multiple wounds incurred in the Bloody Lane at Sharpsburg. Knocked unconscious, Gordon fell face down in his hat and would have drowned in his own blood if a Union bullet had not perforated his headgear and drained the fluid.

Shortly after 3 p.m. Gordon's 1,500 men crept slowly forward through a wheat field bordering the western side of the Harrisburg Road. Shielded by tree cover ahead of them, the Georgians passed the Josiah Benner farm and then splashed across the creek. As his screaming men surged up the knoll, Gordon, mounted on a majestic black charger, stood up high in his stirrups and exhorted the troops with "a voice like a trumpet."

The attackers quickly overwhelmed the Union defenders. Soon the infantrymen of the Eleventh Corps joined masses of their First Corps comrades in the race to reach Cemetery Hill. Gordon reported: "The enemy made a most obstinate resistance until the colors on portions of the two lines were separated by a space of less than 50 paces, when his line was broken and driven back...in the greatest confusion, and with immense loss in killed, wounded, and prisoners." The general also related that one of his regimental color-bearers engaged in hand-to-hand combat with a Union standard-bearer.

Although not suffering the severe casualties incurred by many other Confederate brigades on July 1, Gordon still lost nearly a third of his strength as a result of the attack. Colonel Clement A. Evans' 31st Georgia reported 9 killed and 34 wounded. Among the latter was 19-year-old David Adams of the Bartow Guards. While advancing his regiment's colors during the attack on Blocher's Knoll, Private Adams was struck in the left leg just above the knee. Subsequently taken prisoner, he received medical care in Gettysburg and later in Baltimore before being paroled.

Mirroring the feats of his brigade commander the young soldier seemed to have a propensity for surviving severe injuries. Wounded annually each summer from 1862-64, his luck seemed to have run out when a bullet pierced his right lung at Cedar Creek on October 19, 1864. But the indomitable young man pulled through once again and survived a period of captivity before he was released near the end of the war. No worse for the wear, Adams lived until October 12, 1925, one week shy of the 61st anniversary of his fourth wounding.

Sometime near 5 p.m. Robert E. Lee arrived on Seminary Ridge. Seated upon Traveller, his trusty war-horse, the Southern commander witnessed a thrilling scene—the streets of Gettysburg thronged with hundreds of Union soldiers fleeing towards Cemetery Hill. Located a short distance south of the town, this open elevation dominated the surrounding terrain and the road network over which the remainder of the Union army would be arriving. Through his field glasses Lee observed Union troops rallying on the hill. However, due to the limited daylight, the lack of fresh support troops, and the inherent difficulty of maneuvering infantry through the narrow streets, an attack could not be organized that evening.

Despite this setback, July 1 would be recorded as a very fruitful day for the Army of Northern Virginia. Following behind their blood-red banners, the Confederates had badly mauled two Union infantry corps and then taken possession of Gettysburg proper. The hardened veterans felt confident that they could finish the job tomorrow.

July 2, 1863

During the evening of July 1 and at intervals throughout the next day, the balance of the contending armies marched into the Gettysburg area. Both commanders strengthened their positions and contemplated their next moves.

After much deliberation, General Robert E. Lee decided to maneuver a large force upon the left flank of the Army of the Potomac then resting upon Cemetery Ridge. Then by driving northward with a series of trip hammer blows, he hoped to push the defenders off of Cemetery Hill, the keystone of the Union position. Running roughly parallel to Cemetery Ridge, Seminary Ridge would serve as the staging area for the Southern assaults. Two divisions from Longstreet's Corps, which had not participated in the previous day's fighting, would spearhead the attack. Meanwhile, General Ewell was instructed to carry out a diversion against the opposite end of the Union line.

However, it took the Confederates much of the day to jockey into position. By the time they reached the southern flank of the Federal line, Major General Daniel Sickles had advanced his Third Corps from its original position along the southern extremity of Cemetery Ridge to seize the higher ground along the Emmitsburg Road. The center of Sickles' new line was located around Joseph Sherfy's peach orchard. From there it extended northward along the road to near the Nicholas Codori farm, while the left of his line bent to the southeast before terminating near Devil's Den.

Despite the late hour and the intolerable heat, the bloodiest fighting of the three-day battle would take place before the sun descended over South Mountain. As the Southerners launched a series of desperate assaults upon Sickles' isolated troops, Meade countered by rushing reinforcements to threatened sectors. As they had during the previous day, the Confederate color-bearers would find themselves in the epicenter of the combat.

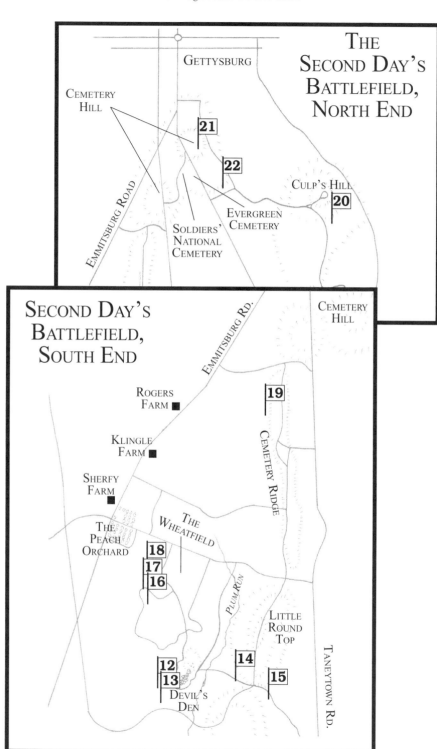

1st Texas
Sergeant George Branard
Robertson's Brig., Hood's Div., Longstreet's Corps

The vital assignment of leading Longstreet's attack upon the Union left fell to the nearly 8,000 combat veterans of Major John Bell Hood's Division. Hood deployed his troops under the cover of Biesecker's Woods in two lines of two brigades each and prepared for action.

At about 4:30 p.m. following a sharp artillery exchange, Hood rode along his front line before halting near his old command, the Texas Brigade, which consisted of the 1st, 4th, and 5th Texas as well as the 3rd Arkansas. The general stood "majestically" in his stirrups and gesturing eastward toward Little Round Top, he shouted, "Fix bayonets, my brave Texans; forward and take those heights!" In response, Lt. Colonel Phillip A. Work, the commander of the 1st Texas, pointed to his unit's state flag and admonished his men to "follow the Lone Star Flag to the top of the mountain!"

After two years of war, the fighting qualities of the Texas Brigade, now under the command of Brigadier General Jerome Bonaparte Robertson, had achieved an almost legendary status. As Colonel Work later explained:

> The success of the Texas regiments was not due to the training of Hood or any other commander, but that they were composed of an intelligent, educated, adventurous and high-spirited people. Infused with the spirit of chivalry, the Texans on every battlefield displayed the sublime, fearless, exalted courage of the heroes of the Alamo and San Jacinto, adoring their Lone Star flag and guarding it with its unsullied record as a dutiful son in the name of an honored father.

Sergeant George Branard
Hill College Collection, USAMHI

Color-Sergeant George A. Branard of the 1st Texas certainly fit this description. Originally the fourth corporal of Company L, "The Lone Star Rifles," and a member of the color guard, 19-year-old Branard received a promotion to color-sergeant on May 11, 1862 after bearing the flag "daringly and gallantly" during the brigade's first experience under fire at Eltham's Landing along the York River. Although intrepid in battle, the former mechanic was also well known for his modesty. One comrade noted that "he was always inconspicuous in camp and disliked ostentation. His was the proverbial timidity of the lamb, and the boldness of the lion."

Early in its history the 1st Texas received the nickname of the "Ragged First" due to its shabby appearance and lack of discipline. Despite this less than flattering sobriquet, the regiment knew how to fight. During Lee's first invasion of the North in September 1862, the Texans caused quite a stir when they marched with Longstreet's Corps through Frederick, Maryland, on the 10th.

A few Confederate partisans voiced their support from among the predominantly pro-Union citizenry. One elderly lady shouted from her home, "The Lord bless your dirty ragged souls!" Spying the unique state flag of the 1st Texas, another bystander exclaimed, "Here comes the Bonny Blue Flag!" Just as Branard passed by one female onlooker a strong breeze caught hold of his flag, wrapping the folds so tightly around the lady that the embarrassed sergeant had to step out of the ranks to "give her time to get out of it."

One week later this carefree hilarity gave way to sheer horror as the 1st Texas lost over eighty percent of its men at the Battle of Sharpsburg, Maryland, the costliest single day of the war. Nine color bearers were shot down and the flag fell into enemy hands. A Union soldier pulled the banner from underneath one lifeless form and counted twelve other corpses nearby.

Remarkably, Sergeant Branard was not among the slain. Having marched from Manassas, Virginia, to Sharpsburg without shoes, his feet were so cut up that he was sent to the rear by the major. Another account states that Branard had been disabled early in the battle and had passed the flag to a member of the guard. Either way he was a lucky man indeed.

After this bloody contest, the 1st Texas recruited new members and received a replacement flag. While Branard was home on furlough in December 1862, six Houston ladies presented him with a miniature First National pattern flag measuring 6 3/4 by 13 1/2 inches with a single star in the canton. Against army regulations, the independent-minded Texan affixed the smaller flag to the staff of his newly issued standard and it was carried this way throughout the rest of the war. Branard and his flags would be in the thickest of the action at Gettysburg.

After descending a gradual slope, the 426 men of the 1st Texas emerged at the base of a rock-strewn, triangular-shaped field. Looming ahead of the Texans on a narrow elevation known as Houck's Ridge stood four cannon supported by a line of blue infantrymen. At the southern end of this elevation lay a massive outcropping of huge boulders. The geological oddity known as Devil's Den was aptly named considering its eerie appearance and the savage, chaotic nature of the fighting that erupted there.

The 1st Texas with the 3rd Arkansas on its left charged up the slope only to be twice repulsed by Union counterattacks. One Texan described the seesaw battle as "one of the wildest, fiercest struggles of the war."

The timely arrival of Brigadier General Henry "Old Rock" Benning's Brigade of Georgians tipped the scales in favor of the attackers by a nearly two to one margin. Following behind the first wave, Benning threw his fresh troops into the heated contest. At first confusion reigned as the various regiments became intermingled in

The miniature flag carried over the regimental colors of the 1st texas.

Museum of the Confederacy, Richmond, Va. Photo by katherine Wetzel the rough terrain. Some of the Georgia infantrymen mistakenly fired into the backs of the Texans. To halt the friendly fire, Branard stepped out into the open and vigorously waved his flag.

Afterward, Branard and the color bearer of the 15th Georgia engaged in a foot race for the summit. The Texan opened up a lead upon his competitor and found himself well in advance of the main body. His gallantry elicited the approval of the Union infantrymen on the ridge as some of them shouted, "Don't shoot that color bearer—he is too brave."

When Union troops finally withdrew from the area, they left behind three guns from Captain James E. Smith's 4th New York Independent Battery. Sergeant Branard sought out the largest rock on the crest near the guns and "planted the adored standard of the Texans, adorned with the Lone Star, shining far off to friend and foe, with the effulgence of its glory." His moment of triumph was short-lived. A Union shell burst nearby, splintering a large portion of the flagstaff, and "hurled the hero unconscious down the slope of the mountain."

One of the fragments had struck Branard in the forehead. Besides inflicting a bloody gash that would leave a permanent scar, the injury destroyed the sight in his left eye and caused hearing loss in his left ear. After reviving a few moments later, the incensed color bearer was determined "to whip the whole Yankee nation by himself."

Obviously, Branard was in no condition to attempt such an ambitious task and for the present the capture of Devil's Den would have to suffice. Although many witnesses later declared that his actions at Gettysburg surpassed any other event that occurred during the war, the Texan "thought nothing of the act and he refrained from alluding to it."

Less than three months later, the color-sergeant was severely wounded in the left arm at Knoxville, Tennessee, incapacitating him for further field duty. After a stint in the ambulance corps, he received a discharge for his disability in February 1865.

Following his marriage to Miss Julia House in 1866, Branard fathered nine children. A lifelong member of Hood's Texas Brigade Association, he carried out the duties of secretary or treasurer for fourteen years. Upon his death in 1909, it was stated that "when the grave closes over him it will hide a shell scar that marked his courage at the time and thereafter till the day of his death."

44th Alabama
Private James L. Forte
Law's Brig., Hood's Div., Longstreet's Corps

Besides Texans, Arkansans, and Georgians, soldiers from Alabama could also boast of their part in the capture of Houck's Ridge. Like the remainder of Brigadier General Evander Law's Brigade, the 363 men of the 44th Alabama were performing picket duty several miles from Chambersburg, Pennsylvania, on the opening day of the battle. At about 3 a.m. on July 2 the brigade received an order to join the army at Gettysburg. After a grueling march of almost thirty miles, the weary infantrymen reached their destination by early afternoon.

Originally posted on the far right of Hood's front line, the 44th and 48th Alabama were shifted to the left to cover a widening gap near the center of the formation. Led by Colonel William F. Perry, the 44th struggled northward up the rocky gorge formed by Plum Run, then burst upon the blue defenders near Devil's Den. Perry described the surreal landscape:

> Large rocks, from six to fifteen feet high, are thrown together in confusion over a considerable area, and yet so disposed as to leave everywhere among them winding passages carpeted with moss. Many of its recesses are never visited by the sunshine, and a cavernous coolness pervades the air within it.

The rugged nature of the ground split the 44th into two wings. As the right portion of the regiment snaked around the imposing boulders, the left wing, under the direction of 24-year-old Major George W. Cary, attacked along the edge of the Triangular Field near the 1st Texas.

During the ensuing charge, the flag was shot down four times whereupon sixteen-year old Private James L. Forte picked it up. The youngster carried the flag to the top of the ridge, where he mounted one of Smith's gun carriages. He triumphantly waved his banner from atop this perch until a Yankee soldier knocked him off. Then with the flag in one hand, Major Cary rushed ahead of his men "with flashing sword and blazing face."

Cary's troops scooped up dozens of prisoners but were soon forced to pull back from their exposed position with the approach of Union reinforcements. Suffering from heat prostration, Colonel Perry paused in a cool recess among the rocks and observed the renewed Confederate assault following the arrival of Benning's Brigade. "The incessant roar of small arms, the deadly hiss of Minnie balls, the shouts of the combatants, the booming of cannon, the explosion of shells, and the crash of their fragments among the rocks, all blended together in one dread chorus whose sublimity and terror no power of expression could compass," marveled Perry.

James Forte survived the carnage only to be killed several months later at the Battle of Chickamauga in northern Georgia. Major Cary overcame a near mortal wound in 1864 and later became a successful businessman. Ironically, the officer who had led a vigorous assault on a New York battery at Gettysburg died in New York City at age seventy, where he was considered "one of the best known and most popular Southerners."

The elation of the Confederates standing atop Houck's Ridge was short-lived. Across the valley 500 yards away the rugged western slope of Little Round Top loomed above them. Near the crest of the hill, which rose 150 feet above the valley floor, an equally ferocious struggle was taking place. From Devil's Den, the scene reminded one Southerner of an erupting volcano. Through the drifting smoke scattered red flags marked the positions of the attacking units. Eventually five Southern regiments, three representing Alabama and two from Texas, opposed Colonel Strong Vincent's Brigade of 1,300 Union troops that had arrived just in the nick of time to prevent the Confederates from occupying the hill. The advantage of position clearly rested with the Federals.

5th Texas
Sergeant T. W. Fitzgerald, Cpl. J. A. Howard, Sgt. W. S. Evans, & Pvt. Andrew Fletcher Robertson's Brig., Hood's Div., Longstreet's Corps

Flanked by the 4th Texas and the 4th Alabama, the veteran soldiers of the 5th Texas scrambled over the northwestern slope of Big Round Top then struggled up the rock-studded precipice of its smaller cousin. "The ascent was so difficult as to forbid the use of arms," recalled the 5th's commander, Colonel Robert Powell. "At last, weary and almost exhausted, we reached the topmost defenses of the enemy," he continued. "Now the conflict raged with wild ferocity. We were caught in a cul de sac or depressed basin, surrounded on three sides by projecting or shelving rocks...."

From their protected lair less than thirty paces away, the Union riflemen fired so rapidly that one soldier in the 5th imagined that he "could hold out a hat and catch it full." He admitted that for the first time in the war the regiment wavered and then drifted backward. The Texans reformed and advanced twice more but failed to dislodge the main enemy line. Lieutenant Colonel King Bryan partly attributed the defeat to the large boulders covering the slope that broke up the regiment's alignment.

The roar of artillery and the rattle of small arms became so deafening during the height of the battle that orders could not be understood even at close range, making the leadership of the color bearer even more vital. Sergeant T. W. Fitzgerald of Company A pressed gallantly forward with the flag until he was severely wounded far in advance of the main line. J. A. Howard, the color corporal from B Company took over and remained firmly at his post until he was killed. Then, Sergeant W. S. Evans, Company F, seized the colors and "planted them defiantly in the face of the foe during the remainder of the fight, always advancing promptly to the front when the order was given."

But not every Civil War soldier enthusiastically took up the colors when the opportunity presented itself. Private William Andrew Fletcher had been offered the honor of carrying his unit's flag at Second Manassas in August 1862. His frank reply was: "I feel I am too cowardly for a flag bearer to risk myself; and I find the oftener I can load and shoot the better able I am to maintain my honor." In reality the modest carpenter from Beaumont, Texas, was anything but a coward. After Fletcher declined the flag at Manassas, a bullet grazed his bowels and lodged in his hip, but he was soon back on duty.

Although only 22 at the time of his enlistment in August 1861, the young man harbored no romantic illusions about warfare. He realized early on that it was a dirty business and he did his share of killing without regret. Fletcher seemed to thrive on excitement. He often volunteered for dangerous scouting missions into enemy territory and often took great risks in battle with the notable exception of carrying the colors.

On July 2 at Gettysburg, Fletcher reluctantly obeyed an order to join the 5th's color guard. During the regiment's repeated attempts to take Little Round Top he saw the colors fall five times, the last time in the hands of the sergeant who had ordered him to join the guard. "In falling, the flagstaff struck my head in front of my face," recalled the private. "As it went down my forward motion caused my feet to become some-what tangled. I gave a kick, said a curse word, and passed on." Fletcher had no idea who picked up the colors afterwards, but he stated unequivo-cally that he had no intention of doing so.

After the wounding of Colonel Powell and Lt. Colonel Bryan, Major Jefferson C. Rogers finally withdrew the regiment from the bloody slope. Upon recovering from a gun shot to the left knee at Camp Letterman Hospital in Gettysburg, Sergeant Fitzgerald returned to active duty only to be shot through the shoulder near Cold Harbor, Virginia, the following summer. This injury confined him to the In-valid Corps for the duration of the war. Sergeant Evans surrendered his life at the Battle of Chickamauga in northern Georgia on Septem-ber 20, 1863.

15th Alabama

Sergeant John G. Archibald &
Sgt. Patrick O'Conner
Law's Brig., Hood's Div., Longstreet's Corps

If Colonel William C. Oates had had his way, he would never have participated in the epic struggle for Little Round Top. Ha-rassed by a contingent of pesky sharpshooters, Oates and his 15th Alabama scaled the thickly timbered western slope of Big Round Top. It was a gruesome way to cap off over thirty miles of march-ing in the space of eleven hours. The intense heat and the difficult ascent left the men panting by the time they reached the summit. Earlier, a detail of 22 men had been sent out to fill the regiment's canteens, but had not returned when the order arrived to move out. Although the party followed the regiment into battle, it be-came lost and stumbled into the enemy lines, thus depriving the 15th's soldiers of a desperately needed commodity.

After halting his weary command, Oates inspected the area and was elated by what he saw. "Within half an hour I could convert it into a Gibraltar that I could hold against ten times the number of men that I had," exclaimed the normally offensive-minded commander. Five minutes later, an officer from General Law's staff rode up and ordered the colonel to press forward without delay and help drive the Union troops off of Little Round Top.

Reluctantly, Oates faced his men to the left and pressed them toward the raging battle. The Alabamians stumbled down the mountainside toward the tip of a rocky spur that overlooked a saddle between the two heights. When the Southerners approached to within fifty feet of this point, the concealed infantrymen of Colonel Strong Vincent's Brigade delivered a destructive volley into their faces. The line staggered, but the gaps closed up and the men instinctively returned fire. One can only marvel at the endurance of the parched Alabama soldiers as they frantically chewed off the ends of their powder-filled paper cartridges with cottony mouths as the acrid smoke hung thickly in the humid air.

Realizing the inherent strength of the enemy position, Oates attempted to swing his force around the left flank of Vincent's line held by Colonel Joshua L. Chamberlain's 20th Maine. In response, the former professor formed his line in the shape of a horseshoe to meet this threat. For over an hour the desperate contest ebbed and flowed around the ledge. Oates later wrote, "the blood stood in puddles in some places on the rocks."

During the last of several charges, the Confederates succeeded in breaching the enemy line until a spirited counterattack drove them back. As hand-to-hand fighting broke out Sergeant John G. Archibald held the colors of the 15th Alabama about forty paces up the slope just to the right of a large boulder. Archibald, a mechanic and painter from Greene County, was 46 years old when he enlisted in Company H, the "Glennville Guards." Despite his advanced age, all of the officers and men of the regiment respected him for his great courage and other good qualities.

Standing within ten feet of the same boulder, Colonel Oates glanced toward the flag in time to witness an incident that impressed him "beyond the point of being forgotten." Civil War soldiers rarely used their bayonets as weapons but any measure would be resorted to when the colors were threatened. As a Maine soldier lunged forward to grasp the staff of the 15th's battle flag, Archibald stepped back and Sergeant Patrick O'Conner, "one of the finest soldiers" in Company K, plunged his bayonet through the head of the brazen Yankee.

Not long afterward, Oates noticed that his dead and wounded were nearly as numerous as the living and he called for a retreat. At the same time, with ammunition running low, the soldiers of the 20th launched a bayonet charge. The weary and stunned Southerners ran "like a herd of wild cattle" as the New Englanders rushed toward them. Overcome by exertion, the husky Oates collapsed during the retreat and would have been captured had not two stalwart soldiers carried him away. William's brother, Lieutenant John Oates, died three weeks later from the effects of several bullet wounds.

Both Patrick O'Conner and John Archibald escaped the clutches of the pursuing Yankees on July 2. In his memoirs, Oates proclaimed that Pat was always at his post and never missed a battle. In recognition the Irish tinsmith received a promotion to lieutenant in December 1863. He was killed six months later at Ashland, Virginia.

Although he suffered severe wounds at two different battles, Archibald carried the battle flag of the 15th until the end of the war. He was promoted to ensign for his gallantry when that rank was created. In his letter of recommendation, Archibald's commanding officer described him as "a brave, cool, and meritorious soldier fully competent for the position, being an able-bodied and healthy man. The appointment could not be bestowed upon a more worthy soldier. His character is beyond reproach."

During the surrender ceremony at Appomattox, the beloved flag bearer tore the colors from the staff and hid them under his shirt. The last time Colonel Oates saw him, Archibald declared that he would keep the old flag until he died and requested that it be placed under his head inside his coffin.

As additional Confederate troops entered the battle, the fighting spread north from Devil's Den and Little Round Top to the area surrounding the Rose Farm. Some of the most savage combat of the battle swirled back and forth across Farmer Rose's twenty-acre wheat field and upon a stony, tree-covered hill that rose from the field's western edge.

8th Georgia

Sergeant Felix H. King, Lt. Melvin Dwinnell, & Cpl. Edward Manis

Anderson's Brig., Hood's Div., Longstreet's Corps

Brigadier General George "Tige" Anderson's Brigade of five Georgia regiments was the last element of Hood's Division to join the attack on the Union left. As the Georgians burst into the open they could see the Lone Star banners of the Texans climbing up the western slope of Little Round Top. Almost immediately, a long line of Union cannon arrayed along the Wheatfield Road near the Peach Orchard poured a murderous fire into the flank of Anderson's formation. The men quickened their pace through the fields and over fences until they reached the protection of a large belt of timber.

The line of advance led the 8th Georgia toward a low swampy area along Plum Run at the southwest edge of the Wheatfield. Lieutenant John C. Reid described it as a bog about twenty or thirty yards across. Protected by large rocks and thick vegetation on the opposite side, Union riflemen let loose with "a scythe of fire" that filled the air with "hissing lead." The Confederates broke into a near-run as they drove home the attack, but the boggy ground proved to be impassable.

Color Sergeant Felix Houston King attempted to lead the regiment across but he became mired down

Lieutenant Melvin Dwinnell,
8th Georgia Infantry.
Courtesy Wes Bradley

in the muck almost up to his midsection. As King struggled to free himself from the morass, a bullet slammed into his leg. Somehow, the 22-year-old sergeant managed to keep the colors up.

Lieutenant Melvin Dwinnell, a 37-year-old native of East Calasis, Vermont, rushed up to King and secured the flag when a missile plowed into his upper left arm. The transplanted Yankee moved to Georgia in 1851 after graduating from the University of Vermont. At the out-break of the war he published the Rome Courier. After Dwinnell's wounding, Corporal Edward Manis of Company H, an "Israelite" from Rome, Georgia, took over as bearer until he fell with a severe wound. Subsequently, other members of the regiment carried the flag, but their names are lost to history.

Lieutenant Dwinnell was disabled for two months after his in-jury near the Wheatfield. He resigned his officer's commission upon being elected to the state legislature in November. King and Manis also recuperated from their wounds. Three of King's brothers served with him in the 8th. Younger brother William died on July 4 after the amputation of his arm and was later buried in Hollywood Cemetery in Richmond, Virginia. Felix King fathered six sons before passing away on Christmas Eve of 1903 near Coosa, Georgia.

The battle flag of the 8th Georgia never fell into enemy hands. Prior to the surrender ceremony at Appomattox, Lieutenant Colonel Edward J. Magruder tucked the cherished banner into his boot and took it home to Rome, where it was used as a cradle quilt for his baby son.

A dignified South Carolina lawyer would lead the opening wave of assaults by Major General Lafayette McLaws' Division. Despite his lack of formal military training, Brigadier General Joseph Kershaw developed into one of Lee's most trusted brigade commanders. For almost two hours his six seasoned regiments hunkered behind a stone wall west of the Emmitsburg Road awaiting the order to join in the growing battle. A field of clover ascended gradually from the base of the wall before falling away toward the road, where a farm lane led to the stone house, barn, and outbuildings of the Rose farm. The Mis-sissippians under the command of fiery ex-politician William Barksdale lined up to the left of Kershaw directly opposite the Peach Orchard. Two brigades of Georgia troops formed a short distance to the rear in support of the lead brigades.

7th South Carolina
Sergeant Alfred D. Clark
Kershaw's Brig., McLaws' Div., Longstreet's Corps

Since artillery projectiles had played havoc among McLaws' waiting soldiers throughout the afternoon, orders were issued not to display the colors during the initial advance. However, as Kershaw's men rose from their prone positions behind the wall just prior to the advance, Sergeant Alfred Clark of the 7th South Carolina thoughtlessly unfurled his flag, perhaps by habit. According to Colonel David Wyatt Aiken, less than a minute later "a shell exploded in his front, killing three and wounding the rest of the color-guard." In another account he stated that the blast killed two men while wounding three others. Whatever the exact figure this incident served as an omen of the horror that would soon follow.

For some reason, the movements of Barksdale and Kershaw were not well coordinated and the result proved disastrous for the South Carolinians. With their left flank unprotected they were exposed to salvos of artillery fire just as Anderson's men had been a short time earlier. But Kershaw's men were within an even closer range.

"We were, in ten minutes or less time, terribly butchered," wrote an officer in the 2nd South Carolina. "I saw half a dozen at a time knocked up and flung to the ground like trifles.... It was the most shocking battle I have ever witnessed. There were familiar forms and faces with parts of their heads shot away, legs shattered, arms torn off, etc."

In light of these horrid conditions the instructions to not display the colors seemed very sensible indeed. Somehow Clarke passed safely through the battle only to lose his life at Chickamauga less than three months later.

3rd South Carolina
Sergeant William P. Lamb
Kershaw's Brig., McLaws' Div., Longstreet's Corps

The Rose property split Kershaw's Brigade into two wings. The three leftmost regiments veered to the left and charged toward the enemy guns south of the Peach Orchard. Meanwhile, the 3rd, the 7th, and the 15th regiments drove straight ahead toward the Stony Hill to link up with Anderson's hard-pressed Georgians.

As the 3rd South Carolina neared the Rose farm buildings, a rabbit bounded out in front of them. In a humorous, but remarkably candid remark, one of the men called out, "Go it, old fellow; and I would be glad to go with you, if I hadn't a reputation to sustain." After initially seizing the hillside from the original group of defenders, Kershaw's troops became embroiled in a hot firefight with Union reinforcements. "I have never seen so much damage done both parties in so short a space of time," declared Colonel David Aiken to his wife.

When four members of the 3rd South Carolina's color guard went down in quick succession, some of the men yelled for Sergeant William Lamb to "Lower the colors, down with the flag." Perhaps feeling the need to sustain his reputation, the sergeant instead stepped to the front where all could see him. As he waved the flag aloft Lamb screamed out loudly in response, "This flag never goes down until I am down." Although he attracted a hail of missiles, Lamb somehow escaped harm.

He was not as fortunate at the Battle of Chickamauga in September when he sustained a severe injury to his right leg. Lamb would be out of action for an entire year. He returned to his home in Laurens, South Carolina, at war's end.

Although late in getting underway, General William Barksdale led his Mississippi regiments in a spirited charge that smashed the Federal line at the Peach Orchard. The advance of McLaws' support line further tipped the balance in favor of the Southerners. Soon Union troops were also driven off the Stony Hill and out of the Wheatfield. Barksdale's victorious troops then veered left toward the remaining Third Corps division that was stationed along the Emmitsburg Road north of the Peach Orchard. At the same time, two brigades from Major General Richard Anderson's Division of Hill's Corps assailed the enemy line from the front.

According to the general plan of attack, the remaining three brigades in Anderson's Division would continue to attack in successive waves from south to north. As the Third Corps infantrymen reeled back with Confederate troops in hot pursuit, Brigadier General Ambrose Wright's Georgia Brigade swung into action.

3rd Georgia

Sergeant Alexander L. Langston,
Capt. Charles H. Andrews,

Adj. Samuel Alexander, Pvt. Thomas J. Hincey,
& Pvt. Edmund J. Horton
Wright's Brig., Anderson's Div., Hill's Corps

Advancing at "quick time" through a hail of artillery projectiles, Wright's Georgians trampled through ripening grain fields and broke down fences until they reached the Emmitsburg Road opposite the Nicholas Codori farm. At this point they received fire from two Second Corps infantry regiments that had advanced from Cemetery Ridge to the east side of the road to support Sickles' troops.

Positioned in the center of Wright's Brigade line, the 3rd Georgia clashed with the 82nd New York just north of the brick Codori house. During this brief encounter, 23-year-old color sergeant Alexander Langston, a 6' 1" tall, blue-eyed farmer from Woodville, Georgia, fell badly wounded. The flag was wrested from his firm clutch by Captain Charles Andrews and Adjutant Samuel Alexander. The Georgians swept aside their opponents, captured two nearby batteries, and then rushed toward a broad gap in the Union line south of a copse of trees, a site that would become famous following the events of July 3.

The troops originally posted to defend this area had been shunted off to other threatened sectors. Wright's men exploited this weakness and established a foothold inside the Federal position. Suddenly, the battle flags of the Georgia regiments waved triumphantly from the ridge crest. General Wright believed that his troops "were now complete masters of the field."

His elation turned to trepidation when he discovered that the brigades to his left had not attacked in concert with his men, leaving the Georgians in a precarious situation. In a matter of minutes, converging Yankee infantrymen, some of them led by General Meade himself, quickly sealed off the penetration. Wright and his command had no alternative but to cut their way out of the closing jaws of the trap.

After being badly wounded, Adjutant Alexander leaned the 3rd Georgia's flag against a captured artillery piece. Many of the Southerners were taken prisoner near the Codori farm as they retraced their steps toward Seminary Ridge. Private Thomas Hincey of Company

H, guarded by his comrade Private Edmund Horton, brought the colors of their regiment off the field.

Five months after the battle, Sergeant Langston succumbed to his wounds. He left no wife or child and was indebted to the Confederate States of America for $12 for clothing.

When Longstreet's men commenced the attack against the Union left, General Ewell opened his demonstration with an artillery barrage against Cemetery Hill. At about 7 p.m., Major General Edward Johnson crossed Rock Creek with three brigades and assailed Culp's Hill from the east. This rugged wooded height located just one-half mile from Cemetery Hill anchored the right flank of the Army of the Potomac.

Ewell's timing could not have been better. By the time he sent his infantry forward, only one brigade from the Union Twelfth Corps remained on the hill to man the breastworks on the eastern and southern slopes. Meade had stripped away the remainder of the troops to shore up his endangered left flank. Although they possessed a strong numerical advantage, Johnson's men would have to struggle up a steep, rock-covered slope as experienced riflemen fired down upon them from the cover of log breastworks.

1st Louisiana
Sergeant Charles Clancy
Nicholls' Brig., Johnson's Div., Ewell's Corps

In the gathering darkness, Johnson's 4,000 troops groped their way along the upper slope of Culp's Hill. Tripping over brush and rocks, the Southerners drove back the Union skirmish line and ascended the hill toward the works held by the 1,350 blue coats in Brigadier General George Sears Greene's five New York regiments.

Francis Nicholls' Louisiana Brigade attacked in the center of Johnson's formation. Due to the wounding of General Nicholls at Chancellorsville, Colonel Jesse M. Williams led the brigade at Gettysburg. Williams reported that his men fought their way to within 100 yards of Greene's main line. For the next four hours they exchanged heavy fire with the New Yorkers and made several unsuccessful attempts to carry the works.

During one of these assaults, Sergeant Charles Clancy, the color bearer of the 1st Louisiana, became separated from his regiment in the shadowy woodlands. Realizing that his capture was imminent, Clancy removed the flag from the staff and hid it under his clothing. He concealed the colors in prison camps until his exchange that winter when he returned to his unit. Reportedly, over two hundred bullets had pierced the flag. Clancy was captured again at Spotsylvania Court House, Virginia, in May 1864. He escaped from Elmira Prison in New York State on December 30.

With the timely assistance of reinforcements, Greene's thin line valiantly held back the Confederate onslaught. However, the Southerners did manage to slip into the unoccupied works on the lower slope of the hill. Later in the evening the remainder of the Twelfth Corps units returned to the hill as four Confederate brigades arrived to reinforce Johnson. The buildup of troops and the proximity of the opposing lines virtually assured the resumption of hostilities in the morning.

Soon after the firing erupted on Culp's Hill, two brigades from General Jubal Early's Division stormed the eastern slope of Cemetery Hill, resulting in one of the rare night actions of the Civil War. General Robert Rodes prepared to support Early with a simultaneous attack upon the other side of the hill. Early's assault force consisted of the 1,200 soldiers of Brigadier General Harry T. Hays' Louisiana Brigade and the 900 North Carolinians of Colonel Isaac Avery's Brigade. Hays' troops emerged from a shallow ravine along the southeast edge of town and advanced toward the base of the hill about 400 yards away. Advancing on the left of the Louisiana regiments, the Tarheels had to traverse an open meadow about four times that distance to reach the enemy position.

8th Louisiana
Private Arthur Duchamp & Cpl. Leon Gusman
Hays' Brig., Early's Div., Ewell's Corps

Although almost universally applied to any infantry unit from Louisiana serving in Lee's army, the fierce-sounding nickname, "Louisiana Tigers," originated early in the war to describe the rowdy behavior of several regiments in the 1st Louisiana Brigade. General

Harry Hays commanded this organization at Gettysburg. Despite their lack of discipline, these men developed into first-class fighters and they earned the fear and respect of their Yankee opponents. Characteristically, Hays' men performed well throughout the summer campaign. The Tigers stormed the main Union fort at Winchester, Virginia, in mid-June and then helped to overwhelm the Eleventh Corps on the opening day at Gettysburg. To these hardened combat soldiers the height of Cemetery Hill certainly looked formidable, but not impossible to carry.

Described as a naturally mild, amiable young man, Private Arthur Duchamp, the color bearer of the 8th Louisiana, did not fit the stereotype of a Louisiana Tiger. But in combat he underwent a transformation, becoming as "brave as a lion" and it was declared that "no man carried his flag closer to the enemy than he did."

From their commanding platform the Union gunners blasted away at Early's men as soon as they popped into view. Fortunately for the Southerners, most of the rounds flew overhead in the growing darkness. The screaming attackers slammed into two weakened brigades from the Eleventh Corps crouched behind a low stone wall at the base of the hill. Pockets of Hays' and Avery's troops punched through at weak spots in the line and rushed up the slope toward the vulnerable batteries near the summit.

The 8th Louisiana struck the Federal line at an angle in the wall. Overwhelmed, the 107th Ohio fell back through the guns of Captain Michael Wiedrich's Battery I, 1st New York Light Artillery. As Private Duchamp led his comrades in a mad rush for these tempting prizes, he fell wounded. Corporal Leon Gusman, a 21-year-old former student, picked up the flag and continued to advance.

Looking behind him, Lieutenant Peter Young, the adjutant of the 107th Ohio, observed the enemy "yelling like demons" among the guns. Realizing that the day might be lost unless the marauders were hurled back, the officer decided on a desperate course to incite his men to a greater effort:

> I ran forward, revolver in hand, shot down the rebel color bearer (8 La. Tiger Regt. as it proved by the inscription on the vile rag) and sprang for the colors, at the same time a rebel, seeing his comrade fall, sprang forward and caught them but fell to the ground, where I wrested them from him. These in one hand and revolver in the other, I was in the act of turning towards our men when a rebel

bullet pierced my left lung and arm.... I kept on my feet till I reached our men when all strength left me and my Sergt. Maj. Henry Brinker caught me in his arms as I was falling.

Young recovered from his injuries, but his adversary Corporal Gusman died on the hill. An Ohio sergeant provided another version of this dramatic story:

> I noticed the color bearer of the Eighth Louisiana Tigers waving his flag near the Battery, and the color-guards massing around on both sides of him. I called the attention of Adjutant Young to this demonstration, and there being about seven of us we at once, by command of the Adjutant, fired a volley and advanced toward them scattering the color-guards in every direction. The color bearer being severely wounded, dropped on one knee holding to his flag with such a firm grip, that Adjutant Young who was trying to wrench it from him could not do it. The color bearer had a large navy revolver in his right hand. I saw him pull the trigger and shoot the Adjutant through the shoulder blade, the Adjutant in turn planted his sabre in the color bearer's breast. The color bearer held on to the flag and sabre with a firm grip until he dropped over dead, never loosening his grip until he drew his last breath.
>
> We made a quick examination of the color bearer's body and found seven bullet holes through him; we also examined the contents of his canteen which, being nearly full, contained whiskey and gun powder, and which we judged accounted for his desperate bravery.

Although the Southerners succeeding in capturing Wiedrich's guns and those of an adjacent battery commanded by Captain R. Bruce Ricketts, it was only a temporary victory. Large numbers of Union reinforcements rushed to the scene and Hays prudently ordered the remnants of the two brigades to retreat.

The men who had participated in the attack grew extremely bitter over the lack of support they received after breaching the enemy position. For some unexplained reason General Rodes did not have his troops in position to attack in concert with Early. The futile attack cost the Confederates about 600 casualties. Attempting to salvage something positive from the calamity, General Hays reported capturing four enemy flags. Predictably, he never mentioned the loss of the colors of the 8th Louisiana.

Private Duchamp survived Gettysburg but his daring exploits eventually caught up with him. One week after being promoted to ensign he was killed at the Battle of Spotsylvania Court House on May 11, 1864, after carelessly exposing himself to place the regimental colors on the earthworks.

21st North Carolina

Major Alexander Miller, Pvt. Jerry W. Bennett, Cpl. Eli Wiley, & Capt. James F. Beall
Avery's Brig., Early's Div., Ewell's Corps

"The hour was one of horror," wrote Captain James F. Beall, who served in the 21st North Carolina. "Amid the incessant roar of cannon, the din of musketry, and the glare of bursting shells making the darkness intermittent...the hoarse shouts of friend and foe, the piteous cries of wounded and dying, one could well imagine... that `war is hell.'" The "maddened column" of Tarheels rushed on toward the Union batteries above them.

Four out of the five North Carolinians who carried the flag that evening gave up their lives. After the death of the first color bearer, Major Alexander Miller picked up the banner until wounded in the breast and arm. He died a month later as a prisoner of war. Stokes County native Private Jerry Bennett retrieved the standard but soon fell dead. Then Captain James F. Beall carried it as the regiment retreated down the hill in the face of Union counterattacks. Corporal Eli Wiley asked permission to take the flag off the field and Beall handed it over to the young soldier. After retreating about twenty-five yards, the captain glanced back to see Wiley being gunned down. In the darkness and confusion the colors remained behind inside the lines of the enemy.

Major Alexander Miller
North Carolina Office of Archives and History

Captain James Beall
North Carolina Office of Archives and History

The following day Private Oliver P. Rood, 14th Indiana, "captured" the flag of the 21st North Carolina for which he received the Medal of Honor. Beall deeply regretted the loss of the colors, but he was even more embittered by Rood's false claim. He noted wryly that the Union private "took the flag from the body of the dead hero who had been cold and stark in death for many hours." In Rood's defense he was certainly not the only individual to receive official recognition for dubious acts of bravery.

The fighting of July 2 ended as the firing gradually sputtered away on the darkened slopes of Culp's and Cemetery Hill. Although it would be the costliest day of the battle as measured by total casualties, no decisive result was obtained. The Union line had been dented or temporarily breached in several spots but still held firm. Lee's attacks were plagued throughout the day by poor coordination among his general officers. On the other hand, Meade and his subordinates seemed to be everywhere; sending fresh troops to threatened sectors at just the right moments.

As the hungry, thirsty, and weary soldiers in blue and gray collapsed upon the ground, they could not have known what a dramatic conclusion the contest would take on the following day.

July 3, 1863

Although Lee had originally planned on simultaneously attacking both flanks of the Union line on July 3, developing events led him to gradually shift his focus toward the Union center, where several of his brigades had nearly broken through during the previous day's fighting. Throughout the morning he refined his new plan of action. Following a massive artillery barrage to soften the enemy position, 12,000 infantrymen would step out from behind Seminary Ridge and advance briskly across a mile of open terrain to punch a gaping hole through the Union line on Cemetery Ridge.

A low stone fence that originated near a copse of trees and ran northward to the Abraham Bryan farm offered some protection for the blue-coated defenders. Just north of the copse, the fence abruptly turned east for a short distance before resuming its northerly course, forming a sharp angle in the line.

Major General George E. Pickett's Division of Longstreet's Corps, about 6,000 strong, was a logical choice to spearhead the infantry attack since it had been held in reserve following its arrival on the field on July 2. Pickett's three fresh brigades formed up in the low ground near Spangler's Woods.

The remaining half of the assault force consisted of eight battered brigades from Hill's Corps. Heth's Division, now commanded by General James Pettigrew, assembled on Pickett's left. The North Carolina brigades of Scales and Lane under the leadership of Major General Isaac Trimble filed into line behind Pettigrew. Two brigades from Anderson's Division were assigned to support Pickett's right.

At about 1 p.m. approximately 170 Confederate guns roared to life. Their Northern counterparts responded and for nearly two hours the earth trembled as screeching and bursting shells filled the air. As the mercury approached ninety, soldiers from both sides clung tightly to the ground and waited out the inferno.

After this fiery ordeal, onlookers from both sides witnessed one of the most magnificent sights of the war. One Confederate soldier who watched the charge from Seminary Ridge never forgot the stirring scene:

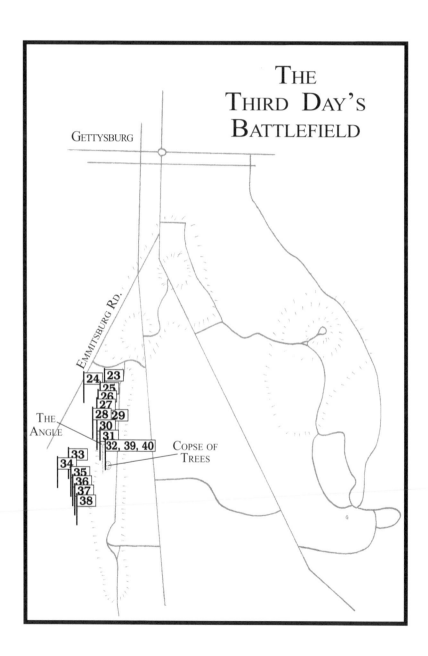

THE
THIRD DAY'S
BATTLEFIELD

GETTYSBURG

EMMITSBURG RD.

24 23
25
26
27
28 29
30
THE
ANGLE
31
32, 39, 40

COPSE OF
TREES

33
34
35
36
37
38

The roar of artillery died on the ear, and our eager lines...advanced under the canopy of sulphurous smoke that densely hung in lowering clouds at the base of the enemy's position. I watched their long lines as they advanced with flying colors, and none but a patriot can realize the emotion that filled my breast, and the thoughts that flitted through my mind. It was a time when hours were compressed into minutes, hearts cease throbbing, and the blood lies dormant in your veins. They are finally hid from view, and then again the terrible rattle of musketry, sounding not unlike the pelting of hail on the housetop, until it finally culminates in a continuous roar that language cannot describe, while the detonating thunder of artillery again sets in and adds new horrors to the bloody drama of death that is going on.

Even the Union soldiers lying in the path of the attack could not help but admire their adversaries. A Connecticut soldier recalled:

All eyes were turned upon the front to catch the first sight of the advancing foe. Slowly it emerged from the woods, and such a column!...extending a mile or more. It was, indeed, a scene of unsurpassed grandeur and majesty.... As far as the eye could reach could be seen the advancing troops, their gay war flags fluttering in the gentle summer breeze, while their sabers and bayonets flashed and glistened in the midday sun. Step by step they came, the music and rhythm of their tread resounding upon the rock-ribbed earth. Every movement expressed determination and resolute defiance, the line moving forward like a victorious giant, confident of power and victory.... There is no swaying of the line, no faltering of the step. The advance seems as resistless as the incoming tide.

But for the Southerners the high water mark was fast approaching. By the time the line reached the Emmitsburg Road it had shrunk to a half-mile in length due to the sweeping fire of the Union artillerists. The survivors rallied on the colors and rushed up the gentle slope of Cemetery Ridge toward the climax of the epic battle.

11th Mississippi

Sergeant William O'Brien, Pvt. Joseph M. Smith, Pvt. William P. Marion, & Pvt. Joseph G. Marable Davis' Brig., Heth's Div., Hill's Corps

When Heth's Division marched toward Gettysburg on the early morning of July 1, the 11th Mississippi remained behind to guard the division's wagon train at Cashtown. By this stroke of good fortune the regiment avoided the fate of the remainder of Davis' Brigade at the Railroad Cut. Rejoining their comrades on July 2, the nearly 600 members of the 11th would more than compensate for their absence by the end of the battle. During the heavy cannonade preceding the July 3 charge, the regiment suffered its first casualties at Gettysburg, but it was a mere prelude to the ordeal through which it would soon pass.

The Mississippians were no strangers to combat. The unit had been present at First Manassas, and participated in all the major battles of the 1862 campaigns. After the thundering guns finally fell silent, the veterans listened intently for the inevitable shout of "Attention!" One officer recalled the tense moments preceding the assault: "The ashen hue that lingered upon every cheek, showed the accuracy with which the magnitude of the task before us was estimated, while the firm grasp that fixed itself upon every musket, & the look of steady determination that lurked in every eye, bespoke an unflinching resolution to `do or die.'"

Soon the command of "Forward" echoed down the double-ranked formation and Davis' infantrymen took their first steps towards Cem-

The battle flag of the 11th Mississippi Infantry

Museum of the Confederacy, Richmond, Va.
Photo by Katherine Wetzel

etery Ridge. The 11th Mississippi was the leftmost regiment in the brigade line. To their left, Colonel John Brockenbrough's small Virginia brigade formed the extreme left of Pettigrew's advance.

As Davis' four regiments neared the Emmitsburg Road, the Virginians fled to the rear after being pummeled by artillery fire from Cemetery Hill and then raked by the spirited rifle fire of the 8th Ohio, which held an advanced position in front of the Union line.

As a result the 11th Mississippi became fearfully exposed to enemy fire from the front and flank. "We were now advancing in the face of a perfect tempest of maddened shells that ploughed our line & made sad havoc in our ranks," wrote Lieutenant William Peel. He continued:

> As we moved onward we were greeted...with showers of...canister, &, at the distance of about two hundred yards the infantry opened on us from behind the stone fence. Pressing onward, we returned the fire. Our line was now melting away with an alarming rapidity. It was already reduced to a mere skeleton to the line of one hour ago. Still on it pushed, with a determination that must ever be a credit to the Confederate soldiery.

Color Sergeant William "Billy" O'Brien numbered among the first casualties. The Ireland-born laborer enlisted in Company C at Okolona, Mississippi, at age 34 near the end of April 1861. He had never missed a battle in which the regiment participated. As O'Brien led his comrades into action on July 3 a shell exploded directly above his shoe tops, propelling his lifeless body skyward in a "macabre dance of death."

Next, a trio of privates from Company H, the "Chickasaw Guards," carried the standard toward Cemetery Ridge. Private James Griffin stooped down to pick up the flag when O'Brien fell dead at his feet, but Private Joseph Smith, a student from Houston, Mississippi, grasped the staff an instant sooner. Standing a shade over five feet, six inches tall, the private with auburn hair and gray eyes had only taken a few steps with the colors when a bullet crashed through his mouth, sprawling him to the ground.

The next bearer, Private William P. Marion, also hailed from Houston and listed his occupation as a student prior to joining the Confederate army. Marion always seemed to be in the thickest of the action. The previous summer he had suffered a head injury and a leg wound within a three week span. As Marion rushed toward the enemy line on Cemetery Ridge he fell dead with the colors.

Joseph Gates Marable then became the final man to raise the banner of the 11th Mississippi on that fateful afternoon. The onetime merchant had already endured much discomfort during his short military career. After being shot in the leg at the Battle of Seven Pines during the 1862 Peninsula Campaign, he was hospitalized with gonorrhea in the fall. The following spring secondary syphilis laid him up for a brief period.

As a knot of Mississippi soldiers closed to within about thirty yards of the Union troops posted near the barn on the Bryan farm, thirteen survivors concentrated around the colors to form an improvised guard. Marable dashed toward the stone fence with "his flag now dangling in graceless confusion" after the staff had been nearly cut in two. He passed through a hail of bullets only to be wounded and stunned as he planted the colors along the barrier.

Both Marable and the colors were captured. Eventually, he and a companion escaped from a Northern prison, and after a series of adventures and hairbreadth escapes, found their way back to the regiment. In recognition of his "gallantry and ability" Marable was promoted to second lieutenant. However, by January 1865 an inspection report listed him as "Absent, sick at home without leave." Perhaps venereal disease proved to be a bigger nemesis than bullets. Joseph's two brothers fought with him at Gettysburg. Younger sibling "Jolly John" Marable was also taken prisoner, while William or "Tip," more than likely his twin, died during the charge.

After being cared for by Union medical personnel, Private Joseph Smith gained his release from captivity by the end of the summer. After additional convalescence in Richmond, he returned to the ranks only to be captured once again near the end of the war. His confinement ended soon after the return of peace.

The 11th Mississippi had the distinction of suffering more casualties on July 3 than any other regiment in the Army of Northern Virginia. The unit lost 103 killed, 166 wounded, and 41 captured, nearly all of these losses being incurred in the space of one hour during the assault. Although the unit's flag presently bears the signature of its captor, Sergeant Ferninado Maggi of the 39th New York, the "Garibaldi Guards," it more deservedly should carry the inscriptions of the four heroes who carried it through the firestorm at Gettysburg.

2nd Mississippi

Sergeant Christopher Columbus Davis
Davis' Brig., Heth's Div., Hill's Corps

By July 3 the proud 2nd Mississippi was a shadow of its former self as a mere 60 men formed in line of battle behind Seminary Ridge. During the debacle at the Railroad Cut two days earlier, the 6th Wisconsin captured 87 members of the regiment, including Corporal William B. Murphy with the regimental flag. Color Sergeant Christopher Columbus Davis had been sick on July 1, but he returned to duty in time to participate in the grand assault. Regarded by his comrades as being "a very brave man, even to recklessness," Davis would certainly do everything in his power to safeguard the new battle flag issued to the regiment by the quartermaster department on July 2.

This recklessness might have stemmed from his difficult childhood. Both of Davis' parents died while he was very young. Consequently, he and his four brothers were raised as orphans. Davis was twenty-one years of age when the war broke out. On April 12, 1861, the day Fort Sumter came under fire from Confederate batteries, the 5' 8" tall, blue-eyed farmer from Pine Grove, Tippah County, enlisted in Company D of the 2nd Mississippi. Wounded and captured at the Battle of Sharpsburg, Davis was exchanged following a three-month imprisonment. He returned to his regiment and was promoted to fourth sergeant on February 16, 1863.

It is likely that the young sergeant marched toward Pennsylvania with a heavy heart. His older brother, Colonel Benjamin Franklin "Grimes" Davis was killed while leading a mounted charge near the beginning of the epic cavalry battle at Brandy Station, Virginia, on June 9, 1863. However, Grimes Davis did not die in a gray uniform. The West Point graduate and veteran Indian fighter maintained his loyalty to the Union despite the fact that all four of his siblings joined the Confederacy. In fact, one of his men wrote that the Colonel "liked to fight the rebels as well as he liked to eat."

A little over three weeks after the death of his brother, Sergeant Davis fell with his second wound of the war as the 2nd Mississippi attacked the Union lines on Cemetery Ridge. Shot through both legs somewhere east of the Emmitsburg Road, he would lie helplessly under the broiling sun as his comrades retreated pell-mell to Seminary Ridge. Somehow, Davis gathered the strength to conceal the colors under his clothing.

Veterans of the 2nd Mississippi gathered around the flag issued to the regiment on July 2, 1863. Although severely wounded, Sgt. Christopher Columbus Davis concealed the colors in his clothing to prevent their capture.

Mississippi Department of Archives and History

During the eerie stillness of the following morning, the prostrate color bearer noticed a mounted officer riding toward him with a captured standard draped over his arm. As the rider drew near, Davis recognized the colors as belonging to his unit. Suffering from shock and loss of blood, he called out in a faint voice, "You have got our colors, let me see them." The Federal officer reined toward him and dismounted.

Ironically, Davis had come face to face with Lieutenant Colonel Rufus Dawes, the commander of the 6th Wisconsin. Dawes had just visited Meade's headquarters at the Leister house seeking permission to send his captured trophy back to Madison. Although his request was denied, the Wisconsin officer was thrilled at the opportunity to speak with a man who identified himself as the color bearer of the regiment that he had fought against just three days earlier. "The poor fellow was quite affected to see his colors," noted Dawes.

The colonel certainly knew that this was not the same man that his unit had captured with the colors near the Railroad Cut, but he was far more concerned about the health of the enemy soldier than he was with verifying his claim. After doing everything in his power to obtain aid and medical attention for Davis, Dawes rode back to Culp's Hill to rejoin his command. He later lamented in his memoirs that he did not know the fate of the Confederate sergeant.

Perhaps it was best that he did not know the end of the story. After his encounter with Dawes, the wounded color bearer was carried to a nearby field hospital. He was eventually relocated to Hammond General Hospital in Point Lookout, Maryland. After recovering from his wounds, Davis took the oath of allegiance to the United States on February 26, 1864. But that June he escaped and returned to his regiment. In recognition of his gallantry, Davis was awarded subsequent promotions to ensign and then to first lieutenant.

Following the war the well-traveled veteran returned home and engaged in teaching, but he never found the inner peace that he so desperately sought. In addition to his older brother Grimes, all three of his siblings that had served in the Confederate service died during the war. A year or two after returning home, the anguish became too much for Davis. "It is presumed that grief at the loss of all his brothers and brooding over the result of the war may have unsettled his reason and suicide was the result," lamented a former comrade. Christopher Columbus Davis was as much a casualty of war as those who had fallen on the field of battle.

26th North Carolina

Sergeant William H. Smith, Pvt. Thomas J. Cozart, Capt. Stephen W. Brewer, & Pvt. Daniel Thomas Pettigrew's Brig., Heth's Div., Hill's Corps

Like the 2nd Mississippi, the 26th North Carolina incurred staggering casualties on the opening day of the battle. The regiment came out with only 216 men from the over 800 that went into action during the attack on McPherson's Ridge. Its beloved colonel was among the slain and one of the fourteen men shot down with the colors.

The battered Tarheels struggled to maintain their discipline and elan as they prepared to march into the jaws of death for the second time in three days. The weather also became a factor as a number of men collapsed from heat exhaustion at the outset of the attack. Despite this adversity, the line moved forward "in as magnificent style as I ever saw," boasted Major John T. Jones, the new commander of the 26th.

However, as the North Carolinians passed through the line of cannon crowning Seminary Ridge, one of the artillerists overheard some of the infantrymen commenting on the strength of the enemy position and expressing doubts over the chances of success. Given the fate of his predecessors, no one could blame Sergeant William H. Smith, the regiment's new color bearer, for being apprehensive.

Captain Stephen W. Brewer
North Carolina Office of Archives and History

The imposing post and rail fences along the Emmitsburg Road proved to be a major obstacle for the troops commanded by Pettigrew and Trimble. Blasts of canister (tightly packed charges of iron balls fired from cannon) and volleys of musketry cut down scores of men as they struggled over these barriers. Seeking protection from the deadly missiles, a substantial number of soldiers took cover along the depressed roadbed and never advanced any farther.

By the time the 26th North Carolina cleared the road the regiment had been "reduced to a skirmish line by the constant falling of men at every step," recalled one of its captains. The remnants of the unit closed on the colors and dashed toward a third fence that extended northward from the Angle.

Three men had already fallen with the colors. Wounded in the head, Sergeant Smith would succumb to his wounds at an area field hospital two weeks later. Then Private Thomas Cozart of Caldwell County died instantly with the ill-fated banner in his hands. Just as they had two days earlier, officers then served as impromptu color bearers. Captain Stephen W. Brewer of Company E enjoyed a reputation of being "brave in battle, gentle in peace, charitable and honorable in all his dealings," and was "beloved and respected by all who knew him." True to his character, he was shot down and badly wounded while carrying the regimental flag.

One of Brewer's men, Private Daniel Boone Thomas, became the final member of the regiment to carry the flag at Gettysburg. Although wounded, Thomas, along with Sergeant James Brooks, made it all the way to the stone fence. Much to their mortification, the pair discovered themselves alone facing hundreds of enemy soldiers. They could not retreat or advance. Observing their predicament some merciful Yankees called out, "Come over on this side of the Lord." Thomas and Brooks crossed the fence and surrendered.

By dark on July 3, the 26th North Carolina consisted of just 67 privates and 3 officers, earning the regiment an unwanted distinction. According to one study, no unit, North or South, lost more men in a single battle throughout the entire war.

Captain Brewer made it back to Seminary Ridge, but was captured near Greencastle, Pennsylvania, on the retreat from Gettysburg. He remained a prisoner until near the end of the war and later became the sheriff of Chatham County, North Carolina. Private Thomas endured the harsh conditions at Fort Delaware prison until he was released in a prisoner exchange in February 1865.

11th North Carolina
Captain Francis W. Bird
Pettigrew's Brig., Heth's Div., Hill's Corps

The 11th North Carolina fought alongside the 26th North Carolina on McPherson's Ridge on July 1, and although not as celebrated as its sister unit, the 11th also incurred heavy losses that day. As a result, a new eight-man color guard was organized

Captain Francis W. Bird
North Carolina Office of Archives and History

for the charge two days later. Fighting by the 26th once again, all eight members of the new guard were shot down. Afterward, Captain Francis W. Bird of Company C, the color company, carried the standard throughout the remainder of the action. Although the staff "had been twice shot off in his hands," the officer returned to Seminary Ridge unscathed. The flag of the 11th North Carolina was the only one from the brigade not to be captured by the enemy.

Bird earned a promotion to major that December and subsequently to lieutenant colonel the following April. He received a mortal wound at the Battle of Ream's Station, Virginia, on August 25, 1864, and died the next day.

5th Alabama Battalion

MAP REF.
27

Private John Bullock, Pvt. Benjamin Manning, & Pvt. Tom Gilbert
Archer's Brig., Heth's Div., Hill's Corps

Archer's small veteran brigade of Tennessee and Alabama regiments constituted the right wing of Pettigrew's force during the grand assault. Following Archer's capture on July 1, Colonel Birkett Davenport Fry of the 13th Alabama assumed command of the brigade. Fry had the vital mission of linking up with Brigadier General Richard Garnett's Brigade, the leftmost portion of Pickett's Division. The flanks of the two commands joined together before reaching the Emmitsburg Road. After clearing the fences, the Confederates pushed through a hailstorm of flying projectiles toward the enemy line.

Small groups from each of Fry's regiments reached the crest of the ridge just north of the Angle. "The line both right and left, as far as I could observe, seemed to melt away until there was but little of it left," reported one of the officers. Receiving no support the survivors drifted backwards. Major A. S. Van de Graaff, the commander of the 5th Alabama Battalion, wrote his wife five days later, "I got within 50 yds. of the breastworks when our line gave way and being completely exhausted lay down in a lane for 15 or 20 minutes, under a very heavy fire. I then ran out, and succeeded in getting back to our line unhurt, although overheated and broken down."

As a member of the battalion recorded in his reminiscences, the color bearers did not fare as well:

The color bearer of the Fifth Alabama is shot down, the flag falls to the ground. Private [John] Bullock of Co. C raises it again. He is shot. Then Private [Benjamin] Manning of Co. B lifts it again and as it floats out on the breeze Manning is killed. Then Private [Tom] Gilbert of Co. A seizes it and succeeds in bearing it to the rear to where we were forced to retreat. This was a bloody charge. Many poor fellows were left stretched upon the field, dead or severely wounded. Four regimental flags were left in the hands of the enemy.

The quartet of captured flags from Fry's Brigade included that of the 5th Alabama Battalion. An officer of the 1st Delaware secured the banner during a counterattack across the stone fence. Somehow the standard eventually came into the possession of Joshua Chamberlain who had commanded the 20th Maine during their defense of Little Round Top on July 2. In June 1943, Miss Rosamond Allen, representing the heirs of Chamberlain, presented the flag to the governor of Alabama.

Shot in the left hip, Private Bullock was admitted to the Episcopal Church Hospital, Williamsburg, Virginia, on September 15, 1863. He was furloughed nine days later.

The battle flag of the 5th Alabama Battalion.

Alabama Department of Archives and History

7th Tennessee
Captain Archibald D. Norris
Archer's Brig., Heth's Div., Hill's Corps

To Lieutenant John H. Moore of the 7th Tennessee the most hazardous part of the advance came along the Emmitsburg Road. He compared the sound of bullets striking the plank fences to "large drops of rain pattering on the roof." The time it took him to climb over the top of the first fence seemed to be "an age of suspense."

Most of Moore's comrades never made it across the road to the second fence. Out of the 47 men in his company, forty lay dead and wounded within a few minutes. "The plank, or slab, fence was splintered and riddled, and the very grass was scorched and withered by the heat of shell and bullets," he wrote. Perhaps only about half of the regiment reached the stone fence that sheltered the enemy. After a brief melee among the rocks, the survivors tumbled back toward the road after doing "all that flesh and blood could do to make the assault successful."

Once again the men had to clamber over the fences under fire and then pass through a gauntlet of open ground before reaching safety. Moore recalled Captain Archibald Norris, whom he considered the best officer in the regiment, "tearing the colors from the staff, and retreating with a fragment of his company under a fire so destructive that his escape seemed miraculous." The other four regiments in Archer's Brigade lost their flags during the charge.

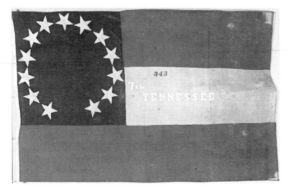

The Stars and Bars pattern of the 7th Tennessee Infantry.

Tennessee State Museum, photo by June Dorman

14th Tennessee

Sergeant Thomas C. Davidson, Sgt. Columbus J. Horn, Cpl. George B. Powell & Borrey Smith Archer's Brig., Heth's Div., Hill's Corps

On July 3 the soldiers of the 14th Tennessee fought against a Union regiment from Connecticut with the same numerical designation. The New Englanders waited anxiously behind the low stone wall that reminded them of those commonly found on farms back home. As their opponents started to cross the fences along the road the order to "Fire!" rang out along the Yankee line. "There opened upon them such a storm of bullets, oaths and imprecations as fully satisfied them we had met before, under circumstances a little more favourable to them...Fredericksburg on the other leg," declared Sergeant Benjamin Hirst, a member of the 14th Connecticut. The regimental historian agreed, stating that "men dropped from the fence as if swept by a gigantic sickle swung by some powerful force of nature. Great gaps were formed in the line...but on they came meeting with the same fate as their comrades."

On the receiving end of the fusillade, Sergeant Robert T. Mockbee of the 14th Tennessee recalled that "the waving battle flags seemed to be the special mark as soon as we came in range of the small arms." Color bearer Thomas C. Davidson from Clarksville, who would later be promoted to ensign for his gallantry at Chancellorsville and Gettysburg, was among those shot down. Before collapsing to the ground, he calmly turned to Sergeant Mockbee and said, "Bob, take the flag, I am shot." Mockbee complied with the request until Sergeant Columbus Horn demanded, "Bob, give me the colors, they belong to Company G." A short time later a bullet blasted him in the face. The Clarksville resident overcame this injury only to be killed at Petersburg near the end of the war.

Mockbee briefly carried the flag again before Corporal George B. Powell of the color guard assumed the duty. Powell fell dead after crossing the road. Mockbee believed that the names of these three men deserved "to appear in letters in Gold in the most conspicuous place in the State House at Nashville."

But the last soldier to carry the colors of the 14th Tennessee that day was perhaps the most intriguing. According to some sources, Borrey or "Bony" Smith may have been a free black or slave fighting

The battle flag of the 14th Tennessee Infantry captured by the 14th Connecticut at Gettysburg.

Tennessee State Museum, photo by June Dorman

in the ranks. Unfortunately, this claim is difficult to verify since many of the blacks who served in Confederate armies did not appear on the regimental muster rolls. Nevertheless, the very possibility that a black man might have carried a Confederate flag into combat must be mind-boggling to modern Americans.

The Connecticut soldiers watched in amazement as the flag bearer of the 14th Tennessee, probably Smith, advanced alone to a low rail fence about ten rods in front of their position. Sergeant Hirst clearly recalled that "he rested his colors before him, then drew himself up to his full height, looking us calmly in the face. There he stood for several awful moments, when the sharp crack of two or three rifles fired simultaneously sent his brave soul to its Maker."

An instant later, several opportunistic soldiers leapt over the wall and dashed toward the undefended flag. Sergeant Major William B. Hincks, a scholarly lad from Bridgeport, outdistanced the competition. With a hearty yell, he seized the staff and ran back with the trophy through a shower of bullets. Hincks received a hearty cheer when he returned to the ranks. Besides the approval of his comrades, he also received the Medal of Honor for his daring feat.

13th Alabama
The Lance
Archer's Brig., Heth's Div., Hill's Corps

The 13th Alabama narrowly averted the loss of its flag on July 1 when flag bearer William Castleberry tore it from the staff and placed it in his "bosom." In his haste Castleberry ripped away the leading edge of the flag and with it the two top eyelets. Afterward, a distinctive replacement staff was fashioned by attaching a lance to the remaining eyelet. When Colonel Fry rode past the regiment on the morning of July 3, he "laughingly commented on the...dangerous looking lance head."

Near the height of the charge Fry fell with a severe wound to his thigh. He was so confident of victory that he sent off the men who had come to his aid by shouting, "Go on — it will not last five minutes longer!" But when the firing ceased loud cheers of victorious Yankee infantrymen reverberated from the ridge.

Lieutenant Colonel Samuel G. Shepard of the 7th Tennessee took over command of the brigade after Fry's wounding. He reported that the 13th Alabama lost three color bearers during the assault, the last one being shot down at the enemy works. Apparently, Color Sergeant Thomas Grant was among them as he received a flesh wound in the right thigh. Captured at Greencastle, Pennsylvania, on July 5, he returned to duty in the fall serving as brigade headquarters courier.

After being captured and taken behind the lines, Fry encountered a Union soldier with an ugly wound in his shoulder that he claimed had been inflicted by a spear attached to the end of a flag staff. Certainly this incident marked one of the few times that the colors of a Civil War regiment functioned as a weapon.

1st Tennessee
Private Wiley Woods
Archer's Brig., Heth's Div., Hill's Corps

Private Wiley Woods carried the flag of the 1st Tennessee into battle on both July 1 and 3. Since his color guard had been decimated on the opening day, Woods improvised to form a new one. As his unit charged toward Cemetery Ridge, he asked three of his com-

Private Wiley Woods and the battle flag of the 1st Tennessee Infantry were
both captured by the enemy on July 3, 1863.

Tennessee State Museum, photo by June Dorman

rades to keep an eye on him and to take the colors if he fell. In quick
succession all three were killed or wounded.

Positioned on the far right of the brigade line, the 1st Tennessee
struck the Federal line at the angle in the stone fence as the troops
posted there began to drift backwards. Some of the remaining
bluecoats called out "we surrender." When no one in authority replied, Woods instructed the soldiers to "crawl over to our side & you
shant be hurt."

Upon the order of acting commander Captain Jacob Turney,
Woods and his fellow soldiers crossed the fence. Turney planned to
have his men fire down the length of the enemy line as he waited for
Trimble's command to come to his assistance. But when the main
line of the North Carolinians evaporated near the road, the captain
reluctantly ordered his small contingent to pull back.

Woods was overtaken by a "little yank" to whom he agreed to
surrender his colors. After escorting his prisoner a short distance
to the rear, the soldier disappeared briefly. Almost immediately, a
pair of Federals approached Woods demanding his flag. Even when
threatened at bayonet point, the Tennessean refused to comply stat-

ing that the colors had already been promised to a man "who was brave enough to cross the wall for them and I intended he should have them."

The original captor soon returned and Woods promptly delivered the standard to him. A nearby officer told this enlisted man that "he did not know how to carry that rag, to trail it in the dust." After his act of chivalry had been tarnished by this humiliating insult, Woods was led away with his fellow prisoners.

While the attacks of Pettigrew and Trimble ground to a halt, Pickett's men had the good fortune of striking the weakest portion of the Federal line at the Angle and in front of the Copse of Trees. Each of Pickett's three brigadiers commanded five regiments. The troops commanded by Richard B. Garnett and James Kemper formed the initial line of attack while Lewis Armistead's men formed the support line. Throughout the assault these veteran soldiers behaved magnificently. As the enemy artillery cut huge swaths in their well-ordered lines they coolly performed a difficult series of maneuvers to close up on Pettigrew's troops. Could the Virginians save the day for the Army of Northern Virginia?

28th Virginia

Sergeant John Eakin, Colonel Robert Allen, and Lieutenant John A. I. Lee
Garnett's Brig., Pickett's Div., Longstreet's Corps

Shortly after forming a connection with Fry's troops on their left, the soldiers of Richard Garnett's Brigade closed in upon the Codori farm and entered the most lethal phase of the attack. One officer used vivid imagery to convey the horrors faced by his command:

> As we approached the Emmitsburg Road, distant about 300 yards from the entrenchments, the storm of lead and iron seemed to fill the air, as in a sleet storm, and made one gasp for breath; and I noticed that many of the men bent in a half stoop as they marched up the slope, as if to protect their faces, and dodge the balls...the hill had suddenly become a volcano, exploding deadly gases, and vomiting fire and destruction upon the valley below.

Lieutenant Thomas C. Holland, 28th Virginia, recalled marching through the "valley of death." One private in the regiment feared that the entire regiment would be killed. General Garnett shouted above the tumultuous roar, "Faster, men, faster! We are almost there!" An instant later, he fell dead from his horse.

Color Sergeant John Eakin received three wounds as he rushed toward the stone fence near the Angle. After a bullet struck him in the upper arm, he finally relinquished the flag to a comrade named Graybill, who advanced only a few steps before being shot dead. This soldier could have been either Lieutenant James Anderson Graybill or Corporal Madison Graybill, both of Company K.

Colonel Robert C. Allen, commander of the 28th, picked up the standard only to be knocked down with a mortal head wound near the fence. Somehow, he handed off the flag to Lieutenant John A. I. Lee of Company C. The 24-year-old farmer from New Castle in sparsely populated Craig County, Virginia, was no stranger to this duty. Before being commissioned as an officer near the end of 1862, he had previously served in the color guard for over a year, six months as the color sergeant.

After receiving the colors from the dying Colonel Allen, Lee earned the distinction of being the first man from Pickett's Division to enter the Union lines. As the 28th Virginia forged ahead of the other regiments in Garnett's Brigade, the Union defenders in their front pulled back and reformed a short distance to the rear. Lieutenant Lee sprang over the low wall "waving the old flag which had heartened the men in so many battles" until a shell knocked it out of his hands.

After he fell with a slight wound, the dauntless officer retrieved the broken standard and attempted to break his sword to prevent it from falling into enemy hands. A Union soldier described as a "big burly German" commanded Lee to surrender, but a nearby comrade stabbed the would-be captor with his bayonet. Another Yankee soon stood over the Confederate officer. Lee must have been shocked by the bedraggled appearance of the man who placed the tip of his bayonet just inches from his chest demanding, "Throw down that flag, or I'll run you through."

Confederate soldiers were habitually destitute, but the grueling campaign had also been hard on their Union counterparts. Although barefoot and wearing a torn and soiled frock coat and trousers, Private Marshall Sherman of the 1st Minnesota could not pass up the

Private Marshall Sherman, 1st Minnesota, with captured colors of the 28th Virginia, circa 1864.

Courtesy of the Minnesota Historical Society, photo by Joel Whitney "opportunity of depriving the Rebs of the stimulus of their colors." The "ragged and blackened" private received the wild applause of his comrades as he passed to the rear with the captured banner of the 28th Virginia and his 5' 9 1/2" prisoner with gray eyes, dark hair, and dark eyes. Sherman's bold act brought an end to Lee's fighting days. After being held in a series of prisons, the Southern officer was finally released on June 12, 1865.

As Lee was being led away, Colonel Allen breathed his last breath. His final thoughts concerned the fate of his flag — "whar was the colors?" he asked. Actually, a portion of the 28th Virginia's flag would continue to see service. During the close-quarters fighting the staff of the 1st Minnesota's flag had also been shattered. After the battle, the Minnesota infantrymen utilized a splintered section from the Virginia flagstaff to repair their own. To one of the men this event "fore-shadowed the time when Union and Confederate should unite in upholding the colors of the old Union forever."

During the 50th anniversary celebration of the battle a former member of the 28th Virginia was attempting to locate his quarters when he stumbled into the tent occupied by Captain Thomas Pressnell and several other veterans of the 1st Minnesota. After learning of the Confederate's unit affiliation, Pressnell informed him that they had captured his regiment's flag at Gettysburg and that it was now in St. Paul. They invited their former adversary to spend the night with them. Before departing the next morning, the Virginian remarked, "I'm sorry we lost that flag, but if we had to lose it, I'm glad it was you fellows who got it."

19th Virginia

Unknown

Garnett's Brig., Pickett's Div., Longstreet's Corps

Forming the center of Garnett's Brigade line, the 19th Virginia assailed the Union line in front of the Copse of Trees. After both the colonel and lieutenant colonel went down, Major Charles S. Peyton took command of the regiment. As the Virginians closed to within twenty paces of the stone fence, Peyton recalled that the line "recoiled under the terrific fire that poured into our ranks both from their batteries and from their sheltered infantry."

After troops from Kemper's and Armistead's brigades arrived in support, the various regiments "rushed forward with unyielding determination and an apparent spirit of laudable rivalry to plant the Southern banner on the walls of the enemy," wrote Peyton. "His strongest and last line was instantly gained," he continued, "the Confederate battle-flag waved over his defenses, and the fighting over the wall became hand to hand, and of the most desperate character; but more than half having already fallen, our line was found too weak to rout the enemy.... Yet a small remnant remained in desperate struggle...until nearly surrounded."

The 19th Massachusetts was among the wave of Union reinforcements that rushed toward the chaotic scene to help seal off the Confederate breakthrough. The historian of this unit vividly remembered the savagery of the fighting and that "the mass of wounded and heaps of dead entangled the feet of the contestants."

As Private Benjamin Falls neared the western edge of the copse he spotted what he believed to be an abandoned flag stuck into the ground on the opposite side of the stone fence. As Falls peered over the fence, however, he discovered a wounded Confederate soldier stubbornly holding on to the staff. The Massachusetts private raised his musket with bayonet fixed over the enemy soldier demanding, "Hut,

Private Benjamin Falls, the captor of the 19th Virginia's battle flag, with the colors of the 19th Massachusetts.

History of the Nineteenth Regiment,
Massachusetts Volunteer Infantry

Tut! Let alone of that or I'll run ye through." Falls led both the "Johnnie" and the colors of the 19th Virginia to the rear, one of four banners captured by the New England boys that afternoon.

8th Virginia
Sergeant William O. Thomas
Garnett's Brig., Pickett's Div., Longstreet's Corps

The 8th Virginia entered the action of July 3 with roughly 200 officers and men but fewer than twenty avoided death, injury, or capture during the course of the bombardment and charge. This casualty rate ranked as the highest percentage loss incurred by any unit on either side at Gettysburg.

Holding the right flank of Garnett's battle line, the 8th passed directly through the Codori farm and became intermingled with elements of the 3rd Virginia of Kemper's Brigade. As the Southerners rushed up the slope a long sheet of lightning unloosed from the low fence near the summit and tore through the compact formation. Private Randolph A. Shotwell pointed out that "at 40 paces it was almost impossible for the poorest of the Yankee marksmen to avoid hitting some one of the advancing throng." He was soon surrounded by comrades "weltering in their life-blood, some on their faces, some on their backs, some writhing and moaning, others still forever!"

Shotwell claimed that half of the division's battle flags dropped after the first volley crashed into the lines. Color Sergeant William O. Thomas held aloft the flag of the 8th Virginia. Standing six feet tall with dark hair and blue eyes, Thomas cut an impressive figure. He had been appointed to his post after being wounded in the thigh during the Peninsula Campaign. According to Shotwell's account: "The flag of the Eighth Virginia fell four times in as many minutes, carrying down a life each time. New men picked it up and carried it on at a full run."

Although a handful of soldiers from the 8th penetrated the Union position, the regimental flag was shot down and abandoned several hundred feet in front of the Copse of Trees. After the battle a member of the 16th Vermont picked up the bloodied standard.

Sergeant Thomas did not perish at Gettysburg, but his army career spiraled downward following the climactic battle. Reduced in rank by court-martial in January 1864, he was off duty on sick leave by the end of the year. Then on March 14, 1865 as Confederate fortunes slowly faded during the siege of Petersburg, Thomas' name appeared on the list of those absent without leave. A little over a month later, he received a parole from Union occupation forces at Winchester, Virginia.

3rd Virginia

Private Joshua Murden, Sgt. William Gray, &
Sgt. Robert A. Hutchins
Kemper's Brig., Pickett's Div., Longstreet's Corps

Perhaps no other brigade in the Confederate army suffered as heavily during the July 3 artillery bombardment as James Kemper's men. Lying behind the crest of Seminary Ridge near a large concentration of Colonel Edward Porter Alexander's guns, the helpless infantrymen were pummeled by counter-battery fire from Cemetery Ridge and Little Round Top. At the height of the barrage General Longstreet boldly rode in front of the lines seemingly oblivious to the danger. Kemper approached his gallant superior to inform him that his troops occupied "a terrible place" and that "a man is cut to pieces here every second while we are talking." Although greatly distressed by this news, Longstreet informed his brigadier to hold out a little longer as the infantry attack would soon get underway.

The 3rd and 7th Virginia regiments were particularly hard hit. Private David Johnston of the 7th Virginia could never erase the horrible scenes from his memory:

> There was to be seen at almost every moment of time guns, swords, haversacks, human flesh and bones flying and dangling in the air or bouncing above the earth, which now trembled beneath us as shaken by an earthquake. Over us, in front of us, behind us, in our midst and through our ranks, poured solid shot and bursting shell dealing out death on every hand; yet the men stood bravely at their post in an open field with a blistering July sun beating upon their unprotected heads.

A shell struck near Colonel Joseph Mayo, the commander of the 3rd Virginia, and splattered his shoulder with a gory mix of soil, blood, and brains. As the terrific artillery duel finally slackened, General Pickett rode briskly down the line calling out, "Up men, and to your posts! Don't forget today that you are from Old Virginia!"

As Colonel Mayo passed among his troops prior to the advance he observed a heartrending sight. His color bearer, Private Joshua Murden, a former mechanic and native of Princess Anne County, was "lying there stark and stiff, a hideous hole sheer through his stalwart body." His right hand was closed in a death grip around the staff of

The Copse of Trees from the Confederate perspective.

the beautiful new cotton bunting flag that had been issued to the regiment three days earlier at Chambersburg, Pennsylvania. Murden became the first man to die defending the flag that "braved the battle and the breeze" for the first and last time that afternoon.

After performing a difficult series of left oblique maneuvers to maintain contact with Garnett's men, the brigade zeroed in on the Copse of Trees. The 3rd Virginia held the left flank of the formation with the 7th on its right, the 1st in the center, and the 11th and 24th on the far right. Besides being subjected to a murderous fire from the front, devastating volleys poured into Kemper's exposed right flank after Brigadier General George J. Stannard swung his 1,900-man Vermont brigade into a firing line perpendicular to the charging Virginians.

As men fell by the scores, Kemper, who was mounted throughout the advance, rose up high in his stirrups, pointed to the left with his sword, and shouted, "There are the guns, boys, go for them." An instant later, a bullet pierced the general's groin and he fell into the arms of his orderly, Private George T. Walker. The badly wounded Kemper was eventually carried back to safety.

Obeying their commander's "injudicious order," the Virginians rushed toward the Federal defenders. After Sergeant William Gray of Company C was shot down with the colors of the 3rd Virginia, Company B's Sergeant Robert A. Hutchins carried them to within twenty yards of the stone fence before he fell wounded.

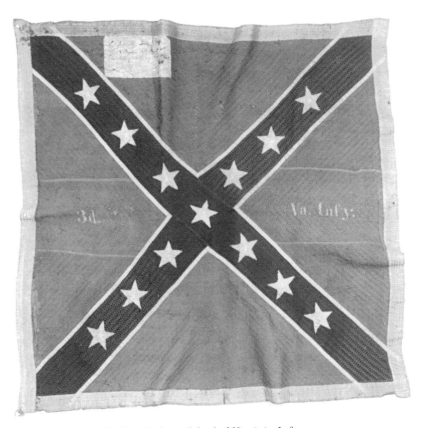

The battle flag of the 3rd Virginia Infantry.
Museum of the Confederacy, Richmond, Va. Photo by Katherine Wetzel

Hutchins was born in Portsmouth, Virginia, in 1842 and had been serving as an apprentice to a ship builder at the Gosport Navy Yard when he joined the army on April 20, 1861. The young sergeant was captured on July 3 and sent to a Northern prison, but he secured his release on January 22, 1864, after taking the oath of allegiance to the United States. Following the war, Hutchins settled back in Portsmouth and gained employment as the city collector.

A soldier from the 71st Pennsylvania remembered how Captain Alexander McCuen of his regiment captured the standard of the 3rd Virginia near the stone fence: "I think he had a little argument with the color bearer, in other words he cut his head off with a sabre and took the colors with him." The short but bloody combat record of the shiny new banner was finally complete.

7th Virginia

Sergeant George W. Watson, Cpl. Jesse B. Young, & Cpl. John N. Tolbert
Kemper's Brig., Pickett's Div., Longstreet's Corps

The officer corps of the 7th Virginia was so decimated on July 3 that by the close of the fighting, command of the regiment devolved upon Captain Alphonso N. Jones of Company K's Madison Grays. In his after action report, Jones wrote, "Its ranks were thinned at every step, and its officers were being rapidly cut down, but this did not check their steady advance which was pressed forward till our flag was planted upon the breastworks of the enemy."

The flag's initial custodian was Color Sergeant George Watson, a 5' 9" blue-eyed student from Madison County. After Watson fell wounded, the members of the color guard continued to advance the flag toward Cemetery Ridge. Corporal Jesse B. Young became the eighth man to carry the standard that afternoon. Young closed to within a few feet of the enemy line before a shell fragment caught him on the right arm and sent him sprawling to the ground. A Federal officer raised his pistol and took aim at Young's head. At the last moment Young threw up his arm to cover his head and the bullet struck him in the elbow instead.

Meanwhile, Corporal John Tolbert, who a comrade described as "a mere boy of ours," seized the flag and carried it to the stone fence. When a projectile grazed his scalp the colors tumbled over the wall and were quickly carried away by an enemy soldier. Both Young and Tolbert returned to duty after brief periods of incarceration at Northern prisons. Young had the distinction of being wounded in action once every summer from 1862-1864.

1st Virginia

Sergeant William M. Lawson, Sgt. Patrick Woods, Cpl. John Q. Figg, Pvt. Willie Mitchel, Pvt. Theodore Martin, & Pvt. Jacob Polack
Kemper's Brig., Pickett's Div., Longstreet's Corps

James Lawson Kemper survived his dreadful wounding at Gettysburg and went on to become governor of Virginia. A decade after the war, Kemper wrote the following of the 1st Virginia, a unit recruited largely from the Richmond area: "You know I was identified with the First through many bloody vicissitudes. Jollier men in camp, braver soldiers in battle were not found in the Army of Northern Virginia."

However, many of the 200 members of the "Old First" who lined up for the charge on July 3 were more concerned with self-preservation than with patriotic fervor. Lieutenant John Dooley expressed this sentiment candidly, "When you rise to your feet as we did today, I tell you the enthusiasm of ardent breasts in many cases ain't there, and instead of burning to avenge the insults of our country, families and altars and firesides, the thought is most frequently, Oh, if I could just come out of this charge safely how thankful would I be!"

When the order was issued to start forward, Color Sergeant William M. Lawson of Company H stepped four paces to the front of the regimental battle line with the colors. The former clerk had performed this sacred duty since May 20, 1862. His color guard consisted of four men that day: Corporal John Figg, Private Theodore Martin, Sergeant Patrick Woods, "a most reckless, daring Irishman," and seventeen-year-old Private Willie Mitchel.

Mitchel, a son of an exiled Irish patriot and onetime student at the University of Paris, tumbled to the ground with a wound at roughly the midpoint in the advance. Nonetheless, he insisted on remaining with the guard. After marching about one hundred yards farther he was killed.

As the line drew close to the stone fence, Pat Woods was shot through the body as Martin and Figg went down nearby in quick succession. Sergeant Lawson's right arm was badly shattered and the colors fell from his hand among the dead and dying. Holland native and University of Leyden graduate Jacob R. Polack rushed into the vortex to retrieve the colors, but he also fell wounded. The flag was left on the ground to eventually be retrieved by an enemy soldier.

The following day about 25 men of the Old First answered roll call. Jacob Polack, who had somehow escaped capture, numbered among the group. Although his left arm was in a sling and his "somewhat prominent nose damaged from the attention of the enemy," he procured a stand of colors from the baggage train and commenced waving them vigorously. This flag had been left lying upon the field at Second Manassas by a South Carolina unit and was picked up there by the Virginians. However, the little band from the 1st was in no mood for such a martial display. They declined to play color guard and induced Polack to cease his demonstrations.

That same day a squad of four men searching for the wounded between the lines recovered the body of Willie Mitchel. His remains were discovered near the Codori farmhouse wrapped in a blanket. The young man's face had been washed and a slip of paper pinned to the blanket. With the assistance of a black man the party dug a grave "on the banks of a small cabin so close that no plow would ever disturb it." Discovering a cracked board nearby, they fastened the slip of paper to it and created a makeshift headstone. After the passage of ten months, Mitchel's mother was finally located and told the site of her son's grave.

Amazingly, the remaining members of the regimental color guard survived the battle and the war. Released through an exchange on March 16, 1864, Pat Woods was appointed to the rank of ensign four months later. Sergeant Lawson's mangled arm was amputated near the shoulder joint. After a brief stay at a prison hospital, he reported back for duty before his stump had fully healed, earning him a promotion to second lieutenant for gallantry. Captured at Sayler's Creek on April 6, 1865, during the retreat to Appomattox, Lawson was set free from Johnson's Island Prison in Ohio on June 9. He died on May 27, 1910. John Figg and Theodore Martin were also taken prisoner at Sayler's Creek. After the war, Figg resided in Baltimore while Martin relocated to Brooklyn, New York.

The battle flag of the 1st Virginia Infantry.
Museum of the Confederacy, Richmond, Va. Photo by Katherine Wetzel

11th Virginia

Sergeant Martin Van Buren Hickok, Adj. Hilary Valentine Harris, & Pvt. George T. Walker
Kemper's Brig., Pickett's Div., Longstreet's Corps

The colors of the 11th Virginia fell three times as the regiment advanced through the small valley between the Emmitsburg Road and Cemetery Ridge located south of the Codori farm. One of these bearers was apparently 26-year-old Martin Van Buren Hickok, who earned an appointment to color sergeant after being wounded in action twice during the 1862 campaigns. As canister rounds cut large swaths in the line, Hilary Valentine Harris, the 24-year-old regimental adjutant, retrieved the standard and carried it forward.

Like the other regiments in Garnett's and Kemper's Brigades, the 11th lost cohesion as it neared the Union position. Captain John Holmes Smith described the formation as "a mass, or ball, all joined together without company organization." Members of adjacent units mingled with those of the 11th, thus adding to the confusion.

Many of the troops on the right of Kemper's Brigade line sought cover in the undulating, brushy ground south of the Copse of Trees. Smith became extremely hopeful when the Yankee regiment in his front began to fall back. At any moment he expected to see the rest of Lee's army "marching up to take possession of the field." His heart sank when he looked back and saw nothing but dead and wounded men and horses in the fields between his position and Seminary Ridge.

Smith realized that he lacked the manpower to stave off a Union counterattack. General Kemper's courier, George "Big Foot" Walker, "a long-legged, big-footed fellow," was sent back for reinforcements. When no help materialized, Smith, who now commanded the regiment, ordered the men to retreat by scattering into small groups to lessen their chance of injury.

Upon returning from his errand, Walker found everybody around the colors of the 11th Virginia shot down. He sprang from his horse, snatched up the flag, remounted, and then galloped towards the Union line. Although his horse was shot down on the way and his clothing pierced by numerous bullets, Walker succeeded in planting the regimental flag near the enemy works. Its final fate and current location are unknown.

Adjutant Harris, who apparently abandoned the flag, passed safely through the hail of fire during his unit's withdrawal. The prewar banker was killed in action a week prior to Lee's surrender at Appomattox. He was buried in the family cemetery at Mill Quarter Plantation in Powhatan County, Virginia.

Sergeant Hickok recovered from his Gettysburg injuries only to be shot in both thighs near the close of the war. Despite his numerous wounds, he lived until April 1913, just three months prior to the 50th anniversary of the Battle of Gettysburg.

53rd Virginia

Sergeant Leander C. Blackburn, Cpl. James T. Carter, Cpl. John B. Scott, Adolphous Johnson, Pvt. Robert Tyler Jones, & Lt. Hutchings Carter Armistead's Brig., Pickett's Div., Longstreet's Corps

Following the maiden engagement of the 53rd Virginia at Seven Pines, Virginia, in the spring of 1862, Colonel B. L. Farinholt recalled an amusing incident concerning the regimental colors:

> Our color sergeant — who claimed to be an old Mexican veteran, but was much doubted ever to have smelled gunpowder — under the first scathing fire of the enemy rapidly retired in disorder to the rear; and in his excitement, when halted by one of our captains and forced back to the front, swore that "he was going to do his duty and take care of that silken banner," which he had promised the ladies who had presented it to the regiment he would do, and he was "not going to have it shot all to pieces in that way."

The color guard of the 53rd would know no such dishonor on July 3. Rather, the regimental flag would play a prominent part in the legendary closing act of Pickett's Charge.

Shortly after the cannonade, the command, "Attention, battalion!" rang out along Armistead's line. The men jumped to their feet and scrambled to their proper places as coolly as if they were preparing for a dress parade. Brigadier General Lewis A. Armistead posted himself in front of the 53rd Virginia, his center regiment and thereby the battalion of direction. Turning to Color Sergeant Leander C. Blackburn, Armistead pointed to Cemetery Ridge and asked the sergeant if he was going to plant his colors on the enemy works. "Yes,

Private Robert Tyler Jones
Confederate Veteran

sir, if God is willing," snapped Blackburn. In another version he answered, "I will try, sir, and if mortal man can do it, it shall be done." Whatever the exact response, it pleased Armistead, for he then shared his flask with the color bearer.

Private Robert Tyler Jones, a grandson of President John Tyler, served in the 53rd's color guard. According to Jones, Armistead drew his sword and in his stentorian voice, exclaimed, "Men, remember what you are fighting for! Your homes, your firesides, and your sweethearts! Follow me!" Often a cold and strict disciplinarian, the Virginia officer had not yet gained the respect of many of his men, but on this day he would win their hearts.

With the next command, "Right shoulder, shift arms, Forward, march" the column stepped off at quick time (approximately 82 yards per minute) toward the Emmitsburg Road. Throughout the advance Armistead kept 15 or 20 steps in front of his brigade just ahead of the colors of the 53rd Virginia. As hissing and screaming shells fell among the troops, Armistead calmly encouraged his men, "Steady, men! Steady!"

Apparently it was not God's will for Sergeant Blackburn to reach the enemy position. A shell tore through his body and he later died at an area field hospital. Lieutenant Colonel Rawley W. Martin took the standard from the dying sergeant, urging the men forward until a member of the color guard relieved him of the duty.

By the time the brigade reached the Emmitsburg Road, Garnett's and Kemper's troops were exchanging fire at close range with the enemy. Feeling a burst of nostalgia, a line officer from the nearby 14th Virginia exclaimed, "Home, home, boys! Remember, home is over beyond those hills!" Stepping over the dead and wounded, Armistead's soldiers had closed to within 75 yards of the stone fence when the general barked out, "Forward, double quick!" and the pace accelerated.

At some point during the advance Armistead had placed his slouch hat on the tip of his sword. One witness remembered:

> The sword pierced through the hat, and more than once it slipped down to the hilt, and we saw it above the naked steel. As often as the hat slipped down, the old hero would hoist it again to the sword's point. And so, borne aloft with matchless courage, it caught the eye, it nerved the hearts of his devoted men, a standard as glorious, as worthy to be sung, as the plume that floated at Ivry above the helmet of Navarre.

The colors of the 53rd Virginia proved equally inspiring. Recalled Lieutenant Colonel Martin: "The men fell like stalks of grain before the reaper, but still they closed the gaps and pressed forward through that pitiless storm...their field and company officers have fallen; color bearer after color bearer has been shot down, but still they never faltered."

During one of these occurrences Corporal James T. Carter reached for the fallen colors, but Corporal John B. Scott snatched them out of his hands. An instant later, Scott fell dead and Carter was wounded. Adolphous Johnson, a member of Company H, the Brunswick Guards, was among the last members of the color guard to take the flag, an act that cost him his life.

As the 53rd dashed toward the Angle, Robert Tyler Jones had possession of the colors. Despite being wounded in the arm, he continued onward. Realizing that his men needed all the inspiration they could get to face the tempest of musketry fire, Armistead yelled over, "Run ahead, Bob, and cheer them up!" Waving the flag triumphantly over his head, Jones leapt upon the wall. A bullet grazed his head and he fell faint from the loss of blood.

Then Armistead turned to Lieutenant Colonel Martin and said, "Colonel, we can't stay here." In reply, Martin cried, "Then we'll go forward." With his hat still on the tip of his sword, Armistead called out, "Follow me, boys; give them the cold steel." Remnants of all three brigades followed the commander as he clambered over the stone fence. Lieutenant Hutchings Carter seized the colors from Jones, and with Armistead by his side he penetrated to the rear section of Lieutenant Alonzo Cushing's guns. It would be among the three flags carried to the farthest point within the Union lines.

Hopes of victory quickly faded as onrushing Yankee infantrymen lapped around the flanks of the little band of Southerners. Hand-to-hand combat ensued and shots were exchanged at such close range that powder burns marked the flesh and clothing of the victims. Two bullets struck Armistead as he placed his hands upon one of the artillery pieces. Shortly afterward, Colonel Martin's left leg was shattered by a bullet.

On the ground bleeding from two wounds, Private Jones remained defiant. Brandishing his pistol, he threatened to shoot the first man that surrendered. Lieutenant Carter had little choice in the matter. Seventeen bullet holes had pierced his clothing after he took charge of the regimental banner, but he somehow did not receive a scratch. Alone and surrounded by Yankees, he surrendered himself and the flag.

Out of the ten men in the 53rd's color guard, Jones and Corporal Carter were the only two to survive the charge. Private Jones later earned a promotion to ensign for his gallantry. He greatly appreciated the commendation but felt it "did me more honor than I deserved."

Armistead was the only one of Pickett's three brigadiers to cross the stone fence. During the entire distance from Spangler's Woods to the Angle, Armistead remained close to the colors of the 53rd Virginia. His actions in those 1,300 yards forever endeared him to the men of his brigade. Tragically, he would never again command them in battle, dying July 5 at a Union hospital. Rawley Martin described his conduct as "an example of patriotic ardor, of heroism and devotion to duty which ought to be handed down through the ages."

The marker in front of the Union cannon designates the point where General Armistead fell mortally wounded on July 3, 1863.

57th Virginia
Sergeant John D. Hutcherson
Armistead's Brig., Pickett's Div., Longstreet's Corps

Another of the Confederate banners to be planted inside the Angle on July 3 belonged to the 57th Virginia. Sergeant John D. Hutcherson of Company G had served as the regimental color bearer since its organization in the summer of 1861. He was wounded in the thigh at Malvern Hill at the end of the Peninsula Campaign but returned to duty in time for the Gettysburg Campaign.

Company and regimental organization were nonexistent by the time Armistead's men reached the front. A deep mass of mixed troops concentrated near the outer angle of the stone fence. A soldier in Garnett's Brigade described the welcome arrival of these reinforcements as "a muffled tread of armed men from behind, and then a rush of trampling feet." Then, after roughly 100 men followed Armistead into the Union lines, pandemonium reigned supreme. "Men fired into each other's faces; there were bayonet thrusts, cutting with sabers, hand-to-hand contests, oaths, curses, yells, and hurrahs."

In the hellish confusion Sergeant Hutcherson was shot and killed. An unknown soldier picked up his flag and continued onward. Colonel John Bowie Magruder, the commander of the 57th, went down with a mortal wound within twenty steps of Cushing's guns, his last words to the regiment being, "They are ours!"

At that moment, however, the 19th Massachusetts and other adjacent regiments swarmed into the area. Carrying both the national and regimental colors of the 19th, Sergeant Benjamin Jellison rushed into the fray. Approaching the pocket of Virginians, one of Jellison's comrades pointed to a Rebel flag and hollered, "Let's get it." Jellison lost contact with his accomplice soon afterward. Despite being heavily burdened with his own flags, he somehow managed to secure the flag of the 57th Virginia and a large number of prisoners to boot.

Indeed at least 38 Confederate battle flags fell into the hands of the Army of the Potomac during or shortly after Pickett's Charge. This staggering total reveals the outcome of the contest. The Southerners fought with characteristic bravery and tenacity, but on this occasion the odds were simply too great, their adversary too determined. Of the roughly 12,000 men who stepped off from Seminary Ridge on July 3 as part of the main assault force, more than half were killed, wounded, or captured. As one Virginian later expressed his disappointment, "We gained nothing but glory and lost our bravest men." Many of these men died for and around their colors.

Epilogue

The grand infantry charge of July 3 started and ended within the space of about an hour. Singly and in small groups the battered Confederate regiments reassembled on Seminary Ridge. One intrepid soldier from the 24th Virginia was still not fought out. Clutching one of the two battle flags retained by his division, he called to General Pickett, "General, let us go it again."[1] His commander, however, was visibly shaken following the bloody repulse of his troops. The sight of General Kemper being carried past in a stretcher moved him to tears.

General Lee and staff then rode upon the scene. The dignified chief displayed as much magnanimity in defeat as he had done following his many victories. Taking his division commander by the hand, he gently consoled him, "General, your men have done all that men could do, the fault is entirely my own." Following a personal encounter with Lee that afternoon, Private Randolph Shotwell observed that there "was an air of sadness, weariness, regretfulness, akin to depression, such as I had never known in him before."[2]

But the Virginian controlled his emotions and prepared his shattered army for an anticipated counterattack. None came and the emergency passed. After three days of intense combat, the Army of the Potomac was in no condition to immediately shift into an offensive mode. Besides, Meade was not willing to carelessly gamble away a long sought after victory on a risky frontal assault over the same terrain.

Throughout the stormy evening of July 4-5, Lee's somber troops stepped out from behind their breastworks and began the long trek back to Virginia. Meade's cautious pursuit got underway the following afternoon. Over the next several days the various elements of the Army of Northern Virginia reached the banks of the Potomac near Williamsport, Maryland. Much to Lee's consternation, recent heavy rains had swollen the river to near flood stage. Having no other recourse, he ordered his veteran soldiers to dig in along the eastern shore.

After a slow and deliberate approach, the Federal infantry deployed on a parallel line opposite the bridgehead. Following a reconnaissance of the enemy position, Meade hesitated to launch a full-scale assault on the formidable Confederate defenses. The river began to recede during this delay and on the evening of July 13 the Southerners quietly slipped across to the Virginia side.

Heth's Division remained behind to cover the main crossing point at Falling Waters, a small town a short distance southwest of Williamsport. In the morning probing Union horsemen launched a mounted charge against the Confederate rear guard and nearly cut it off from the remainder of the army. Although Heth's men eventually fought their way back to the pontoon bridge spanning the river, the blue troopers gathered up hundreds of prisoners. In the confusion, a bullet extinguished the life of General James J. Pettigrew, who had survived the carnage of July 1 and 3 at Gettysburg.

Brockenbrough's Virginia Brigade, which turned in dismal performances on both the opening and final days of the battle, surrendered three regimental flags to the enemy. Sergeant Charles M. Holton, a member of the 7th Michigan Cavalry, recorded his capture of one of these colors:

> Seeing the color sergeant of the Fifty-fifth Virginia fall wounded, I sprang from my horse and seized the colors. As I remounted, I heard the wounded color bearer say: "You Yanks have been after that old flag for a long time, but you never got it before." ...General [Judson] Kilpatrick examined the captured flag, and found on it the names of all the great battles of the Army of Northern Virginia. The guard ordered me to join his staff with it for the balance of the day, and in the evening Adjutant Briggs wrote an inscription on the margin of the flag, telling how it had been captured by me.[3]

Another flag lost during the retreat from Gettysburg was the homemade blue silk banner carried by the Bedford Southside Dragoons, a volunteer company of men later designated as Company F, 2nd Virginia Cavalry. Hand-painted by local women, a large portrait of George Washington adorned one side of the flag while the Virginia state seal appeared on the reverse. The slogan "State Rights" and the state motto, "Sic Semper Tyrannis," were also included. An ex-Dragoon recovered the lost standard in 1919 in Trenton, New Jersey, later turning it over to the local chapter of the United Daughters of the Confederacy. The Bedford County Museum, Bedford, Virginia, is currently raising funds to restore this historic artifact.[4] All told the Army of the Potomac netted over 60 enemy flags during the campaign, a feat it would not come close to replicating until the end of the war.[5]

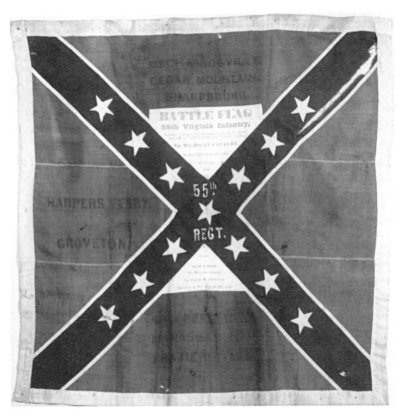

The battle flag of the 55th Virginia Infantry captured by Sgt. Charles Holton of the 7th Michigan Cavalry near Falling Waters.

Museum of the Confederacy, Richmond, Va. Photo by Katherine Wetzel

With the advantage of hindsight, modern historians can point to the battle of Gettysburg as a major turning point in the Civil War. However, for the soldiers and civilians of 1863 it only ushered in a new phase of unimaginable carnage. In the spring of 1864 the outnumbered Army of Northern Virginia tenaciously slugged it out with the reorganized and well-equipped Federals, personally directed by Lieutenant General Ulysses S. Grant, the commander of all Union armies.

Brutal clashes erupted at the Wilderness near the old Chancellorsville battlefield and immediately afterward at Spotsylvania Court House. Despite suffering horrendous losses, the Union invaders kept circling to the southeast, compelling Lee to fall back towards the Confederate capital at Richmond. In early June, Grant ordered a costly frontal assault against a firmly entrenched position at Cold Harbor, a strategic crossroads situated only ten miles northeast of Richmond. After this bloodletting, the weary combatants settled into grueling siege warfare around Petersburg, Virginia.

Throughout the fall and winter of 1864-65, Grant exerted almost continuous pressure on the thinly stretched Confederate army as he gradually cut off its supply lines to the south. With limited manpower and dwindling resources, Lee could not win this battle of attrition. Deprived of the freedom to maneuver, the strength of his once powerful force was slowly sapped by battle casualties, disease, and desertion.

On April 1, as the siege approached the ten-month mark, the right flank of the Southern line crumbled at Five Forks, forcing Lee to evacuate Petersburg and Richmond 23 miles to the north. Hungry and exhausted, the bedraggled Confederates staggered westward as Grant's legions pursued vigorously.

On the morning of April 9, Lee awoke near the unpretentious little village of Appomattox Court House to find his rapidly melting army bottled up by converging Yankee troops. Realizing that further resistance would be futile, he sullenly rode off to meet Grant and discuss arrangements for surrender. A formal agreement was drawn up in the front parlor of Wilmer McClean's home in the village.

For the proud Virginian, the sharp sting of defeat was partly mitigated by the lenient terms set forth by his adversary. Upon receiving their paroles both officers and men were permitted to return to their homes. Privately owned horses, personal baggage, and officer side arms would not be confiscated. Grant did, however, demand an official ceremony for the collection of muskets, artillery pieces, and other public property, including flags.

On the following day Lee composed his last order as commander of the Army of Northern Virginia. He assured his faithful soldiers that nothing could be accomplished by additional sacrifice and reminded them that they had earned "the satisfaction that proceeds from the consciousness of duty faithfully performed." The general prayed for God's blessing and protection while expressing "an unceasing admiration of your constancy and devotion to your country, and a grateful remembrance of your kind and generous consideration for myself." He then bade them farewell.[6]

The gray skies and damp chill that prevailed on the morning of April 12 matched the solemn mood of the vanquished Confederates, now numbering less than 30,000, as they marched into town to lay down their arms and battle flags. An awed stillness settled over the Union troops lining the streets as they observed close-up the ragged and gaunt, but still proud soldiers who had fought so hard for so long. Lieutenant Colonel Horace Porter, Grant's aide de camp, wrote an account of this touching scene:

> The charges were now withdrawn from the guns, the camp fires were left to smolder in their ashes, the flags were tenderly furled—those historic banners, battle-stained, bullet-riddled, many of them but remnants of their former selves, with scarcely enough left of them on which to imprint the names of the battles they had seen—and the Army of the Union and the Army of Northern Virginia turned their backs upon each other for the first time in four long, bloody years.[7]

Unprecedented suffering and death had long since tempered the patriotism and fiery passions of 1861. But even now, without country or cause to fight for, the Southern soldier's love for his battle flag never wavered. Some of the veterans devised clever means to avoid handing them over to the enemy.

During the flight from Richmond a member of the 4th Alabama picked up a flag that had been thrown onto the street by a frightened civilian. On the evening prior to the surrender ceremony, the remaining members of the 4th spread their old banner upon the ground. "What a picture is presented of those few surviving soldiers, who four years before, had been so hopeful, so joyous, so certain of victory; now in their faded grey uniforms, the agony of abandonment in their faces, they were together for the last time!" recalled Captain R. T. Coles. "After tomorrow there were to be no more long hard marches, no more battles, no more roll calls, the Confederate States of America had ceased to exist! What did they not feel, those men as they surrounded their battle scarred flag!"

Each man in turn stepped forward and tore off a piece of the "sacred relic" and hid it away. The next day the impostor Richmond flag was brought forth from a knapsack and surrendered with the arms of the Alabamians. In explanation of this deception, Captain Coles asked, "Should they surrender this symbol of the principles which had led them into battle? Their comrades had died for it; they had starved and borne unparalleled hardships for it! Surrender It? Never!"[8]

Notes and Sources

Introduction

1. Shelby Foote quoted in Tony Horwitz, *Confederates in the Attic: Dispatches from the Unfinished Civil War* (New York: Pantheon Books, 1998), 153.
2. Interview with Shelby Foote, *The American Enterprise Magazine*, Jan./Feb. 20, 2001, Online Version, 1-2.
3. Shelly Oppel, "Confederate Flag Quietly Removed From Capitol," *St. Petersburg Times*, February 10, 2001.
4. The following articles were used as sources for the flag controversies: Borgna Brunner, "Confederate Flag Controversy," Infoplease.com; Joe Davidson, "Dishonoring America," *Christian Science Monitor*, May 10, 2001; Philip Delves, "Mississippi Vote to Keep Confederate Flag Symbol," *Broughton Daily Telegraph* (UK), April 19, 2001; John Deppen, "Why Should Anyone Hold the Confederate Flag Responsible?" *The Daily Item* (Sunbury, Pa.), February 3, 2002; David Walsh, "50,000 Protest Confederate flag in South Carolina: Political issues in the Fight for Democratic Rights," January 26, 2000, World Socialist Web Site.
5. For a sampling of these cartoons visit Daryl Cagle's Professional Cartoonists Index @ http://cagle.slate.msn.com/news/flag/main.asp.
6. Patrick Jonsson, "Southern pride and T-shirts that divide," *Christian Science Monitor*, August 10, 2001; Deborah Fitts, "Virginia Appeals SVC Flag Ruling," *Civil War News*, December 2001; Deborah Fitts, "Virginia SCV Wins License Plate," *Civil War News*, June 2002.
7. Devereaux D. Cannon, Jr., *The Flags of the Confederacy* (Gretna, LA: Pelican Publishing Company, 1997), 7-13, 51-54; The Editors of Time-Life Books, *Echoes of Glory: Arms and Equipment of the Confederacy* (Alexandria, VA: Time-Life Books, 1998), 230-232.
8. Editors of Time-Life Books, *Arms and Equipment of the Confederacy*, 232-233, 260. The pattern universally referred to today as the Confederate battle flag was a rectangular and borderless version of the Army of Northern Virginia flag that was issued to the Army of Tennessee beginning in 1864.
9. *Arms and Equipment of the Confederacy*, 250; Cannon, 14-24, 31-33.
10. See Cannon, 93-95, for the music and lyrics to this song.
11. *Arms and Equipment of the Confederacy*, 230.
12. Joshua Chamberlain, *The Passing of the Armies: An Account of the Final Campaign of the Army of the Potomac, Based Upon Personal Reminiscences of the Fifth Army Corps* (New York: G. P. Putnam's Sons, 1915), 261-262.

13. James McPherson, *What They Fought For, 1861-1865* (Baton Rouge: Louisiana State University Press, 1994), 48.

14. The average strength of the Confederate regiments engaged at Gettysburg was 330 men. The largest was the 26th North Carolina with 840 members. Conversely, ten Southern regiments contained less than 200 soldiers. John W. Busey and David G. Martin, *Regimental Strengths and Losses at Gettysburg* (Hightstown, NJ: Longstreet House, 1994), 229, 231, 236.

15. For an excellent and detailed discussion of these concepts see Richard Rollins, *"The Damned Red Flags of the Rebellion," The Confederate Battle Flag at Gettysburg* (Redondo Beach, CA: Rank and File Publications, 1997),1-46.

16. Rollins, 77.

17. Michael Dreese, *The 151st Pennsylvania Volunteers at Gettysburg: Like Ripe Apples in a Storm* (Jefferson, NC: McFarland & Co., 2000), 48.

18. Rollins, 77.

19. *Arms and Equipment of the Confederacy*, 235.

20. Gary W. Gallagher, ed., *Fighting for the Confederacy: The Personal Recollections of General Edward Porter Alexander* (Chapel Hill: University of North Carolina Press, 1989), 222.

21. J. F. J. Caldwell, *The History of a Brigade of South Carolinians Known First as "Gregg's," and Subsequently as "McGowan's Brigade"* (Philadelphia: King & Baird, 1866); Reprint, Dayton, OH: Press of Morningside Bookshop, 1974, 95.

22. John M. Coski, "Battle Flag: A Brief History of America's Most Controversial Symbol," *North & South*, Vol. 4, No. 7 (September 2001), 60. This article provides illuminating details on the flag's post-Civil War symbolism.

The Campaign

1. Sallie Brock Putnam, *Richmond During the War: Four Years of Personal Observation* (New York: G. W. Carleton, 1867; Reprint, Alexandria, VA: Time-Life Books, 1983), 222-225; Burke Davis, *They Called Him Stonewall: A Life of General T. J. Jackson, C. S. A.* (New York: Rinehart, 1954), 449-450; John B. Jones, *A Rebel War Clerk's Diary*, 2 vols. (Philadelphia: J. B. Lippincott & Co., 1866) Reprint, Alexandria, VA: Time-Life Books, 1982), Vol. 1, 321.

2. Putnam, 222.

3. Henry Kyd Douglas, *I Rode With Stonewall* (Chapel Hill: The University of North Carolina Press, 1940), 222-223.

4. Edwin B. Coddington, *The Gettysburg Campaign: A Study in Command* (New York: Charles Scribner's Sons, 1968), 4-9; Wilbur S. Nye, *Here Come the Rebels!* (Baton Rouge: Louisiana State University Press, 1965), 3-10.

5. Nye, *Here Come the Rebels!*, 10-11; 13, 43-44.

6. Mark Chance, "Prelude to Invasion: Lee's Preparations and the Second Battle of Winchester," *The Gettysburg Magazine*, No. 19 (July 1998),

34; Archie P. McDonald, ed., *Make Me a Map of the Valley: The Civil War Journal of Stonewall Jackson's Topographer* (Dallas: Southern Methodist University Press, 1973), 153; Terry L. Jones, ed., *Campbell Brown's Civil War* (Baton Rouge: Louisiana State University Press, 2001), 194.

7. *Campbell Brown's Civil War*, 194.

8. George Underwood, *History of the Twenty-sixth Regiment of the North Carolina Troops in the Great War, 1861-'65* (Goldsboro, NC: Nash Brothers, 1901), 39.

9. Wiley Sword, *Southern Invincibility: A History of the Confederate Heart* (New York: St. Martin's Griffin, 1999), 78-87, 156, 159-163; Archie K. Davis, *Boy Colonel of the Confederacy: The Life and Times of Henry King Burgwyn, Jr.* (Chapel Hill: The University of North Carolina Press, 1985), 4, 30, 32-34, 38-40, 46-47, 68-72.

10. Underwood, 3.

11. Fred A. Olds, "Brave Carolinian Fell at Gettysburg," *Southern Historical Society Papers*, 52 vols. (Richmond, VA: Southern Historical Society, 1876-1952), Vol. 34, 322.

12. Henry Burgwyn, Jr. to mother, June 15, 1863, quoted in Davis, *Boy Colonel of the Confederacy*, 272.

13. Sword, 159-160; Davis, 247-248; McPherson, 49.

14. Coddington, 75-76; Nye, 171.

15. Richard L. T. Beale, *History of the Ninth Virginia Cavalry in the War Between the States* (Richmond, VA: B. F. Johnson, 1899), 74-75.

16. Accession Records, The Museum of the Confederacy, Richmond, VA, June 4, 1937; Rebecca A. Rose, Curator of the Flag Collection, The Museum of the Confederacy, to the Author, March 20, 2002. This flag remained in the Tapscott family until it was donated to the museum in 1937.

17. *The War of the Rebellion: A Compilation of the Official Records of the Union and Confederate Armies*, 128 vols. in 4 series. (Washington, DC: Government Printing Office, 1880-1901), Vol. 27, Part 2, 442, 551 (Hereafter referred to as *OR*); Coddington, 162-172; McDonald, 154-155.

18. *Campbell Brown's Civil War*, 201.

19. Henry A. London, "Thirty-second Regiment," in Walter Clark, ed., *Histories of the Several Regiments and Battalions from North Carolina in the Great War, 1861-'65*, 5 vols. (Goldsboro, NC: Nash Brothers, 1901), Vol. 2, 525-526. London served as a private in the 32nd North Carolina. His account of the origins of the regiment's Second National flag differs markedly from Campbell Brown's version. According to London, an elegant flag was fashioned by the ladies of Richmond a few weeks after the Confederate Congress approved the new design. The new banner was then sent to General Lee who would then present it to the most deserving regiment in the army. The flag passed down through the chain of command until the 32nd was "honored and complimented in a most notable and con-

spicuous manner" at Carlisle. The regiment then carried this special standard into battle at Gettysburg. As historian Richard Rollins pointed out, Brown's version was written much closer to the actual event and prior to the battle there were numerous veteran regiments more deserving of this honor than the relatively untried North Carolinians.

20. *Campbell Brown's Civil War*, 201-202.
21. *Ibid.*, 202-203.
22. Clark, 526.
23. Harry W. Pfanz, *Gettysburg - The First Day* (Chapel Hill: The University of North Carolina Press, 2001), 21-28.

July 1, 1863

13th Alabama
William H. Moon, "Beginning of the Battle at Gettysburg," *Confederate Veteran*, Vol. 33 (1925), 449-450; Elijah T. Boland, "Beginning of the Battle of Gettysburg," *Confederate Veteran*, Vol. 14 (1906), 308; W. A. Castleberry, "Thirteenth Alabama — Archer's Brigade," *Confederate Veteran*, Vol. 19 (1911), 338; *OR*, Vol. 27, Part 2, 637.

55th North Carolina
Charles M. Cooke, "Fifty-fifth Regiment," in Clark, Vol. 3, 291-293, 296-297, 302; Weymouth T. Jordan, Jr. and Louis H. Manarin, eds., *North Carolina Troops, 1861-1865: A Roster*, 13 vols. (Raleigh, NC: Division of Archives and History, 1971-1996), Vol. 13, 349, 377, 430; S. A. Ashe, "The First Day at Gettysburg," *Confederate Veteran*, Vol. 38 (1930), 379; Alfred H. Belo, "The Battle of Gettysburg," *Confederate Veteran*, Vol. 8 (1900), 165; Frances H. Casstevens, *The Civil War and Yadkin County, North Carolina* (Jefferson, NC: McFarland & Company, 1997), 47-48, 115-116.

2nd Mississippi
William B. Murphy to F. A. Dearborn, June 29, 1900, Robert Brake Collection, United States Military History Institute, Carlisle Barracks, Pa. (Hereafter cited as USAMHI); Rufus Dawes, *Service With the Sixth Wisconsin Volunteers* (Marietta, OH: E. R. Alderman & Sons, 1890; Reprint, Dayton, OH: Morningside Bookshop, 1984), 166-171; Terrence J. Winschel, "The Colors are Shrouded in Mystery," *The Gettysburg Magazine*, No. 6 (January 1992), 77-80; Lance J. Herdegen and William J. K. Beaudot, *In the Bloody Railroad Cut at Gettysburg* (Dayton, OH: Morningside House, Inc., 1990), 194-202, 208; William J. K. Beaudot, "Francis Ashbury Wallar: A Medal of Honor at Gettysburg," *The Gettysburg Magazine*, No. 4 (January 1991), 16, 18, 20.

5th Alabama
Newspaper Clipping, *Alabama Beacon*, July 24, 1863, 5th Alabama File, Gettysburg National Military Park Library (Hereafter referred to as GNMP); Samuel Pickens Diary, 5th Alabama File, GNMP; Guy W. Hubbs, *Guard-*

ing *Greensboro: A Confederate Company and the Making of a Southern Community* (Masters thesis, University of Alabama, 1999), 242-243.

20th North Carolina

Memoirs of Charles Blacknall, North Carolina Department of Archives and History, copy in Robert Brake Collection, USAMHI; Isaac Hall, *History of the Ninety-seventh Regiment New York Volunteers* (Utica, NY: L. C. Childs & Son, 1890), 138-141; Pfanz, *Gettysburg - The First Day*, 175-176; Rollins, 105-106; Clark, Vol. 2, 119; The Memoirs of Captain Lewis T. Hicks, Company E, 20th Regiment North Carolina Infantry, 20th North Carolina File, Gettysburg National Military Park Library; Jordan and Manarin, Vol. 6, p. 436; "Old Soldiers Defy Gettysburg Heat," *New York Times*, July 2, 1913.

26th North Carolina

Underwood, 47-52, 55, 105-107; R. Lee Hadden, "The Deadly Embrace: The Meeting of the Twenty-fourth Regiment, Michigan Infantry and the Twenty-sixth Regiment of North Carolina Troops at McPherson's Woods, Gettysburg, Pennsylvania, July 1, 1863," *The Gettysburg Magazine*, No. 5 (July 1991), 27-30; Olds, "Brave Carolinian Who Fell at Gettysburg," 320-322; John R. Lane Interview, W. H. S. Burgwyn Papers, North Carolina Department of Archives and History, Raleigh, North Carolina; Albert S. Caison, "Southern Soldiers in Northern Prisons," *Southern Historical Society Papers*, (1895), Vol. 23, 159; Sword, 346-348; Davis, 326-339, 347; Jordan and Manarin, Vol. 7, 479, 547, 560; Rod Gragg, *Covered With Glory: The 26th North Carolina Infantry at the Battle of Gettysburg* (New York: HarperCollins, 2000), 111-112, 116, 117-118, 121, 126, 129-132, 135, 233.

13th North Carolina

Varina D. Brown, *A Colonel at Gettysburg and Spotsylvania* (Columbia, SC: The State Company, 1931), 78; Robert K. Beecham, *Gettysburg: The Pivotal Battle of the Civil War* (Chicago: A. C. McClure & Co., 1911), 80-81; Busey and Martin, 292; John B. Gordon, *Reminiscences of the Civil War* (New York: Charles Scribner's Sons, 1904), 114; Medical Case History File of William F. Faucette, National Museum of Health and Medicine, Washington, DC; William Mark Faucette, *The Descendants of William E. Faucette and Elizabeth Wallis* (Carrollton, GA: William Mark Faucette, 1998), 60-62; Greg Mast, *State Troops and Volunteers: A Photographic Record of North Carolina's Civil War Soldiers*, 2 vols. (Raleigh: North Carolina Department of Cultural Resources, Division of Archives and History, 1995), 183; David G. Maxwell, "The Two Brothers," in Clark, Vol. 4, 405-406; W. G. T. Thompson to "Dear Mother and Sister," July 20, 1863, copy in Robert Brake Collection, USAMHI.

14th South Carolina

Brown, 79-80, 85, 87; John P. Nicholson, ed., *Pennsylvania at Gettysburg: Ceremonies at the Dedication of the Monuments Erected by the Common-*

wealth of Pennsylvania to Mark the Positions of the Pennsylvania Commands Engaged in the Battle, 3 vols. (Harrisburg, PA: William Stanley Ray, State Printer, 1914), Vol. 2, 909; Allan Nevins, ed., A Diary of Battle: The Personal Journals of Colonel Charles S. Wainwright, 1861-1865 (New York: Harcourt, Brace, & World, 1962), 236.

1st South Carolina
Captain Washington P. Shooter to Lieutenant George A. McIntyre, July 20, 1863, copy in The Drumbeat, the newsletter of the South Carolina Civil War Round Table (June 1989), 2-4; Military Service Records of Albert P. Owens and James Larkin, National Archives and Records Administration, Washington, DC (Hereafter cited as NARA); Caldwell, 98-99; Philip Katcher, The Army of Robert E. Lee (London: Arms and Armour, 1994), 120.

14th North Carolina
OR, Vol. 27, Part 2, 587; Clark, Vol. 1, 719; Jordan and Manarin, Vol. 5, 471; Preston Ledford, Reminiscences of the Civil War, 1861-1865 (Thomasville, NC: News Printing House, 1909), 70; William A. Smith, The Anson Guards (Charlotte, NC: Stone Publishing Co., 1914), 200; Diary of John McClendon, William R. Perkins Library, Duke University, Durham, N. C.

31st Georgia
Gregory C. White, "This Most Bloody and Cruel Drama": A History of the 31st Georgia Volunteer Infantry (Baltimore: Butternut and Blue, 1997), 90-94, 300; Gordon, 114; Larry Tagg, The Generals of Gettysburg: The Leaders of America's Greatest Battle (Campbell, CA: Savas Publishing Co., 1998), 262-264.

July 2, 1863

1st Texas
Rollins, 116-118; Garry E. Adelman and Timothy H. Smith, Devil's Den: A History and Guide (Gettysburg: Thomas Publications, 1997), 14, 29-31, 43, 51-52, 118-119; Harry W. Pfanz, Gettysburg: The Second Day (Chapel Hill: The University of North Carolina Press, 1987), 186, 194, 200; George Branard Letter, July 1, 1896, The Museum of the Confederacy, Richmond, VA; Harold B. Simpson, Hood's Texas Brigade: A Compendium (Hillsboro, TX: Hill Junior College Press, 1977), 13; Harold B. Simpson, Hood's Texas Brigade: Lee's Grenadier Guard (Waco, TX: Texian Press, 1970), 162-163, 176-177; Joseph B. Polley, Hood's Texas Brigade (New York: The Neale Publishing Co., 1910), 126-129, 350; Robert Maberry, Jr., Texas Flags (College Station: Texas A&M University Press, 2001), 74-78.

44th Alabama
Adelman and Smith, 36-38; Jack Childers, "Colonel George W. Cary," Confederate Veteran (May 1909), Vol. 17, 242; William F. Perry, "The Devil's

Den," *Confederate Veteran* (April 1901), Vol. 9, 161-162; H. H. Sturgis, "Little Billy Fort," *Confederate Veteran* (September 1922), Vol. 30, 345.

5th Texas
Robert M. Powell, "With Hood at Gettysburg," *Philadelphia Weekly Times*, December 13, 1884; John W. Stevens, *Reminiscences of the Civil War: A Soldier in Hood's Texas Brigade, Army of Northern Virginia* (Hillsboro, TX: Hillsboro Mirror Print, 1902), 114-115; *OR*, Vol. 27, Part 2, 412-414; William Andrew Fletcher, *Rebel Private Front and Rear* (Austin: University of Texas Press, 1954), v-xii, 59-60; Military Service Records of W. S. Evans and T. W. Fitzgerald, National Archives, Washington, DC.

15th Alabama
William C. Oates, *The War Between the Union and the Confederacy and its Lost Opportunities* (New York: The Neale Publishing Company, 206-227, 711, 755-756; Thomas Dejardin, *Stand Firm Ye Boys From Maine: The 20th Maine and the Gettysburg Campaign* (Gettysburg: Thomas Publications, 1995), 57-58, 65-73; F. Key Shaaff to Samuel Cooper, September 8, 1864, Military Service Records of John Archibald, National Archives, Washington, DC.

8th Georgia
Warren Wilkinson and Steven E. Woodworth, *A Scythe of Fire: A Civil War Story of the Eight Georgia Infantry Regiment* (New York: HarperCollins, 2002), 238-241; Diary of John C. Reid, Alabama Department of Archives and History, copy in 8th Georgia File, Gettysburg National Military Park Library; Edward J. Magruder to John Towers, January 19, 1888, and related biographical information found on 8th Georgia Infantry web site compiled by Dave Larson (http://home.earthlink.net/~larsrbl/8thGeorgiaInfantry.html).

7th South Carolina
Mac Wyckoff, *A History of the Third South Carolina Infantry* (Fredericksburg, VA: Sergeant Kirkland's Museum and Historical Society, 1995), 120; David W. Aiken, "The Gettysburg Reunion: What is Necessary and Proper for the South to Do," *Charleston News and Courier*, June 21, 1882; David W. Aiken to Wife, July 11, 1863, copy in 7th South Carolina File, Gettysburg National Military Park Library; Franklin Gaillard Papers, Southern Historical Society Collection, University of North Carolina Library, Chapel Hill, North Carolina; Military Service Records of Alfred D. Clarke, National Archives, Washington, DC.

3rd South Carolina
Wyckoff, 121-124, 271; David W. Aiken to Wife, July 11, 1863, copy in 7th South Carolina File, Gettysburg National Military Park Library; Augustus Dickert, *History of Kershaw's Brigade With Complete Roll of Companies, Biographical Sketches, Incidents, Anecdotes, Etc.* (Dayton, OH: Press of Morningside Bookshop, 1976), 240-241.

3rd Georgia
Charles Andrews, "Another Account of General Wright's Brigade at Gettysburg," *Atlanta Journal*, March 9, 1901; Pfanz, *Gettysburg: The Second Day*, 384-389, 416-421; *OR*, Vol. 27, Part 2, 623-624; Military Service Records of Alexander Langston, National Archives, Washington, DC.

1st Louisiana
Harry W. Pfanz, *Gettysburg: Culp's Hill and Cemetery Hill* (Chapel Hill: The University of North Carolina Press, 1993), 6, 209-217, 441; *OR*, Vol. 27, Part 2, 513; Rollins, *"The Damned Red Flags of the Rebellion,"* 128-129; Military Service Records of Charles Clancy, National Archives, Washington, DC.

8th Louisiana
Terry L. Jones, "Twice Lost: The 8th Louisiana Volunteers' Battle Flag at Gettysburg," *Civil War Regiments*, Vol. 6, No. 3 (1999), 89-97, 103; Terry L. Jones, ed., *The Civil War Memoirs of Captain William J. Seymour, Reminiscences of a Louisiana Tiger* (Baton Rouge: Louisiana State University Press, 1991), 122; Peter F. Young to John B. Bachelder, August 12, 1867, in David L. and Audrey J. Ladd, eds., *The Bachelder Papers: Gettysburg in Their Own Words*, 3 vols. (Dayton, OH: Morningside House, Inc., 1994-1995), Vol. 1, 311.

21st North Carolina
James F. Bealle, "Twenty-first Regiment," in Clark, Vol. 2, 137-138; Jordan and Manarin, Vol. 6, 538, 579, 647.

July 3, 1863

Introduction to Pickett's Charge
J. C. Gorman Letters, 2nd North Carolina File, Gettysburg National Military Park Library; Charles D. Page, *History of the Fourteenth Regiment, Connecticut Volunteer Infantry* (Meriden: CT: The Horton Printing Co., 1906), 151.

11th Mississippi
Steven H. Stubbs, *Duty, Honor, Valor: The Story of the Eleventh Mississippi Infantry Regiment* (Philadelphia, MS: Dancing Rabbit Press, 2000), 428-429, 459-466, 658, 711, 826, 827, 831; Steven R. Davis, "...Like Leaves in an Autumn Wind": The 11th Mississippi Infantry in the Army of Northern Virginia," *Civil War Regiments*, Vol. 2, No. 4 (1992), 293-296, 297; Terrence Winschel, "The Gettysburg Diary of Lieutenant William Peel," *The Gettysburg Magazine*, No. 9 (July 1993), 104-106; Baxter McFarland, "Losses of the Eleventh Mississippi Regiment at Gettysburg," *Confederate Veteran*, Vol. 31 (1923), 258-260; Baxter McFarland, "Casualties of the Eleventh Mississippi Regiment at Gettysburg," *Confederate Veteran*, Vol. 24 (September 1916), 410-411.

2nd Mississippi
Terrence J. Winschel, "The Colors are Shrowded in Mystery," *The Gettysburg Magazine*, No. 6 (January 1992), 77-86; Dawes, 160, 366-367; Edward G. Longacre, *The Cavalry at Gettysburg* (Lincoln: University of Nebraska Press, 1986), 51, 66-67.

26th North Carolina
Gragg, 159-160, 188, 197, 200, 228-229; Underwood, 64, 72; Jordan and Manarin, Vol. 7, 519, 531, 538, 599; Earl J. Hess, *Pickett's Charge — The Last Attack at Gettysburg* (Chapel Hill: The University of North Carolina Press, 2001), 182-183, 204-205, 256.

11th North Carolina
Clark, Vol. 1, 590; Jordan and Manarin, Vol. 5, 6, 32.

5th Alabama Battalion
OR, Vol. 27, Part 2, 647; A. S. Van de Graaff to "My dear wife," July 8, 1863, 5th Alabama Battalion File, Gettysburg National Military Park Library; William Frierson Fulton II, *The War Reminiscences of William Frierson Fulton* (Gaithersburg, MD: Butternut Press, Inc., 1986), 77-79; Curator's Object Files, Civil War Flags, Alabama Department of Archives and History, Montgomery, Alabama; Military Service Records of John Bullock, National Archives, Washington, DC.

7th Tennessee
John H. Moore, "Heth's Division at Gettysburg," *The Southern Bivouac*, Vol. 3 (September 1884-May 1885), 391-393; John H. Moore, "Heroism in the Battle of Gettysburg," *Confederate Veteran*, Vol. 9 (January 1901), 15-16.

14th Tennessee
Robert L. Bee, ed., *The Boys From Rockville: Civil War Narratives of Sgt. Benjamin Hirst, Company D, 14th Connecticut Volunteers* (Knoxville: The University of Tennessee Press, 1998), 150-151; Page, 152-158; Robert T. Mockbee, "The 14th Tennessee Infantry Regiment," *Civil War Regiments*, Vol. 5, No. 1 (1996), 28, 42; Gregory A. Coco, *Confederates Killed in Action at Gettysburg* (Gettysburg: Thomas Publications, 2001), 123-125; 139; Rollins, 180, 207; C. Wallace Cross, Jr., *Ordeal by Fire: A History of the Fourteenth Tennessee Volunteer Infantry Regiment, C.S.A.* (Clarksville, TN: Montgomery County Museum, 1990), 72.

13th Alabama
Birkett D. Fry to John B. Bachelder, December 27, 1877, in Ladd and Ladd, *The Bachelder Papers*, Vol. 1, 517-520; *OR*, Vol. 27, Part 2, 647; Greg Biggs, "Ragged Rags of Rebellion: The Flags of the Confederacy," unpublished manuscript, Curator's Files, Alabama Department of Archives and History, Montgomery, Alabama; Curator's Object Files, Civil War Flags,

Alabama Department of Archives and History; Military Service Records of Thomas J. Grant, National Archives, Washington, DC.

1st Tennessee

Wiley Woods, "The 1st Tennessee Flag at Gettysburg," Confederate Veteran Papers, Rare Book, Manuscript, & Special Collections Library, Duke University, Durham, North Carolina; Jacob B. Turney, "The First Tennessee at Gettysburg," *Confederate Veteran*, Vol. 8 (December 1900), 535-537.

28th Virginia

Kathy Georg Harrison, *Nothing But Glory: Pickett's Division at Gettysburg* (Hightstown, NJ: Longstreet House, 1987), 84-85, 106, 356-357; Frank E. Fields, Jr., *28th Virginia Infantry* (Lynchburg, VA: Howard, 1985), 25-27, 57, 61, 67; Thomas C. Holland, "With Armistead at Gettysburg," *Confederate Veteran*, Vol. 29 (February 1921), 62; Ida Lee Johnston, "Over the Stone Wall at Gettysburg," *Confederate Veteran*, Vol. 31 (July 1923), 248-249; J. G. Hamilton, ed., *The Papers of Randolph Abbott Shotwell*, 2 vols. (Raleigh, NC: North Carolina Historical Commission, 1929-1931), Vol. 2, 13; Rollins, 170-172; Michael A. Dreese, *Never Desert the Old Flag! 50 Stories of Union Battle Flags and Color-Bearers at Gettysburg* (Gettysburg: Thomas Publications, 2002), 98; "Old Soldiers Defy Gettysburg Heat," *New York Times*, July 2, 1913.

19th Virginia

OR, Vol. 27, Part 2, 386; Harrison, 105; Rollins, 168; Ernest L. Waitt, *History of the Nineteenth Regiment, Massachusetts Volunteer Infantry, 1861-1865* (Salem, MA: The Salem Press Company, 1906), 246.

8th Virginia

Hamilton, Vol. 2, 13-15; Randolph A. Shotwell, "Virginia and North Carolina in the Battle of Gettysburg," *Southern Historical Monthly*, 112-115, copy in 8th Virginia File, Robert Brake Collection, USAMHI; John E. Divine, 8th Virginia Infantry (Lynchburg, VA: Howard, 1986), 22-25, 83.

3rd Virginia

Lee A. Wallace, Jr., *3rd Virginia Infantry* (Lynchburg, VA: Howard, 1986), 37-38, 56, 92, 98; Joseph C. Mayo, "Pickett's Charge at Gettysburg: Graphic Story," *Southern Historical Society Papers* (1906), Vol. 34, 328-332; David E. Johnston, *Four Years a Soldier* (Princeton, WV: Privately Published, 1887), 271-272; Harrison, 24-25, 65-69; Hess, 153-155; Rollins, 173.

7th Virginia

Report of Alphonso N. Jones, July 5, 1863, copy in 7th Virginia File, Robert Brake Collection, USAMHI; Johnston, *Four Years a Soldier*, 263; David E. Johnston, *The Story of a Confederate Boy in the Civil War* (Ann Arbor, MI: University Microfilms, 1972), 215; David F. Riggs, *7th Virginia Infantry* (Lynchburg, VA: Howard, 1982), 26, 96, 98, 101.

1st Virginia
Lee A. Wallace, Jr., *1st Virginia Infantry* (Lynchburg, VA: Howard, 1984), 43-44, 62, 93, 102, 105, 107, 111, 123; Joseph T. Durkin, ed., *John Dooley, Confederate Soldier* (Washington, DC: Georgetown UP, 1945), 104-105; Charles T. Loehr, "The 'Old First' Virginia at Gettysburg," *Southern Historical Society Papers* (1904), Vol. 32, 36; Charles T. Loehr, *War History of the Old First Virginia Infantry Regiment Army of Northern Virginia* (Richmond, VA: William Ellis Jones, 1884), 38; Harrison, 46-47, 73, 100, 149.

11th Virginia
Robert T. Bell, *11th Virginia Infantry* (Lynchburg, VA: Howard, 1985), 40, 77, 78; Johnston, *Four Years a Soldier*, 257-258; Rawley Martin and John Holmes Smith, "The Battle of Gettysburg and the Charge of Pickett's Division," *Southern Historical Society Papers* (1904), Vol. 32, 191-192; Harrison, 71-72; Hess, 230, 269; Rollins, 227.

53rd Virginia
F. B. Farinholt, "Battle of Gettysburg — Johnson's Island," *Confederate Veteran*, Vol. 5 (1897), 467-469; James T. Carter, "Flag of the Fifty-third Virginia Regiment," *Confederate Veteran*, Vol. 10 (June 1902), 263; James E. Poindexter, "General Lewis Addison Armistead," *Confederate Veteran*, Vol. 22 (November 1914), 503-504; Robert Tyler Jones, "General L. A. Armistead and Robert Tyler Jones," *Confederate Veteran*, Vol. 2 (September 1894), 271; Martin and Smith, "The Battle of Gettysburg and the Charge of Pickett's Division,"186-187; Maude Carter, The History of Pittsylvania County, Va., excerpt in 53rd Virginia File, Robert Brake Collection, USAMHI; "The Brunswick Guards," *Southern Historical Society Papers* (1903), Vol. 31, 124; Rollins, 166.

57th Virginia
Rollins, 176, 226-227; Charles W. Sublett, *57th Virginia Infantry* (Lynchburg, VA: 1985), 66; Johnston, "Over the Stone Wall at Gettysburg," 249; Harrison, 91, 115, 117; W. F. Beyer and O. F. Keydel, *Deeds of Valor: How America's Civil War Heroes Won the Congressional Medal of Honor* (Detroit: Perrien-Keydel, Co., 1903), 236.

Epilogue
1. Loehr, *War History of the Old First Virginia*, 38.
2. Shotwell, 116.
3. Beyer and Keydel, 255.
4. "CSA Flag Restoration," *The Civil War News*, June 2002.
5. Rollins, 224-229.
6. National Park Service, *Appomattox Court House* (Washington, DC: U. S. Government Printing Office, 1980), 105-106.
7. Joseph P. Cullen, "The Reestablishment of Peace and Harmony," in *Appomattox Court House*, 78-79.
8. Alice V. D. Pierrepont, *Reuben Vaughan Kidd* (Petersburg, VA: Violet Bank, 1947), 376-377.

About the Author

The author at the monument to the 11th Mississippi Infantry featuring Color Sergeant William O'Brien.

Michael A. Dreese was born and raised in Freeburg, Pennsylvania. After graduating from Selinsgrove High School in 1981, he received an Associate Degree from Williamsport Area Community College. Mike serves on the advisory committee of the Seminary Ridge Historic Preservation Foundation. He has been recognized by the Gettysburg Battlefield Preservation Association and the Pennsylvania House of Representatives for his contributions to historical preservation.

The primary focus of Dreese's research and writing has been the first day's battle at Gettysburg and the human saga of the Civil War. He is the author of *An Imperishable Fame: The Civil War Experience of George Fisher McFarland, Like Ripe Apples in a Storm: The 151st Pennsylvania Volunteers in the Gettysburg Campaign,* and *The Hospital on Seminary Ridge at the Battle of Gettysburg.* Dreese is a regular contributor to the Gettysburg Experience and his articles have also appeared in *Gettysburg Magazine, Military Images, North & South, America's Civil War* and *Bucknell World.*

Mike is employed by the U.S. Postal Service in Lewisburg, Pa., and resides in Kreamer, Pa., with his wife Heather, and two children, Brooke and Shane.

THOMAS PUBLICATIONS publishes books about the American Colonial era, the Revolutionary War, the Civil War, and other important topics. For a complete list of titles, please visit our website at:

www.thomaspublications.com

Or write to:

THOMAS PUBLICATIONS
P.O. Box 3031
Gettysburg, Pa. 17325